# Emotional Healing in Minutes

**Simple Acupressure Techniques for Your Emotions**

Valerie Lynch and Paul Lynch

Thorsons

Thorsons
*An Imprint of* HarperCollins*Publishers*
77–85 Fulham Palace Road,
Hammersmith, London W6 8JB

The Thorsons website address is:
www.thorsons.com

First published 2001

10  9  8

© Valerie Lynch and Paul Lynch

Valerie Lynch and Paul Lynch assert
their moral right to be identified as the
authors of this work

A catalogue record for this book
is available from the British Library

ISBN 0 00 711258 0

Printed and bound in Great Britain by
Martins the Printers Ltd,
Berwick-upon-Tweed

## Disclaimer

We do not recommend substituting these techniques for the professional services of a
doctor, psychiatrist or psychologist. Please consult your medical health professionals
regarding the use of this treatment. Readers who are under medical supervision should
consult their own medical practitoner before treating themselves or others using the
procedures outlined in this book. Do not use these techniques to try to solve a problem
where your common sense would tell you it is not appropriate. Please take full
responsibility for your own emotional and physical well-being when using this technique.
We make no guarantees that EFT will work for everybody and there are no claims of cures.

# Contents

# Acknowledgments

Firstly, we would like to acknowledge Gary Craig for developing The Emotional Freedom Technique and for making it so accessible to others.

Above all our love and thanks to Karrie-Anne Bish who expressed our thoughts and ideas into the written word, making this book possible. A personal thank you to each individual who so kindly shared their story with us, in the hope that others may be helped. We would like to express our gratitude to Lindsey Kirkbright for her advice and guidance throughout and Keith Marshall whose red pen was greatly appreciated.

We are extremely grateful to our family and friends for their on-going support, love, patience and encouragement. We would also like to acknowledge everyone who has inspired and helped us along the way.

To all who read this book, we wish you love, light, peace and happiness.

# Foreword

Gratitude to Paul and Val Lynch for this highly useful version of EFT. They have combined the power of the EFT procedure with their own innovations to creatively portray an easy-to-apply technique that is useful to almost everyone. Please study this loving work carefully as many of its concepts are life changing. Use it, practise it and pass it on to others. The world will be a better place for your efforts.

Gary Craig, Founder, Emotional Freedom Techniques (EFT)

# Preface

Emotions are beautiful and creative energies and without them life would be extremely dull. We would function as nothing more than robots, devoid of all feeling. Depression is often described in the same way, as a condition in which everything feels flat and emotionless.

A healthy emotional life leads to a fulfilling and meaningful existence, rich with colour and experience. Our emotions make us aware that we are alive; they represent a pure expression of our deepest self. Emotions by their very nature cannot lie. They continually communicate with us, inspiring us and filling us with passion. From the moment of our conception to the time of our death we experience emotions. They are essential to our psychological growth and play an essential role in our well-being.

Feelings attract our attention, indicating the desirable and non-desirable elements in our lives. They illustrate the things we find pleasurable, rewarding and that make us happy, as well as the circumstances that do not. When we feel joy and happiness we are encouraged to move towards those people, situations or environments that produce these feelings. When we experience emotional pain, it signifies the need to remove ourselves or stop whatever it is that makes us so miserable. By listening to the message our emotions send, we are guided in the direction that needs to be taken.

Emotions are our true teachers, healers and guides. For instance, appropriate anger alerts us to the possibility that our boundaries have been broken. We may need to assert our needs more visibly or defend our position. Fear is designed to protect us and guide us away from threatening situations. Through grief we begin the process of adjusting to our painful loss and so allow healing to take place. It is through our emotions that we evolve, change and mature.

Emotions are fluid, moving energies that encourage us to be transformed – e-motion = energy in motion. When we express our emotions naturally, we continue to grow, expand and develop into more of our own inner potential. By staying in touch with our true selves, we become balanced and healthy individuals with the ability to function and cope with the demands that life places upon us.

Not all emotional experiences are pleasant. Some people feel very uncomfortable with the torrent of emotion that flows through them, preferring instead to take solace in the 'safety' of logic and reason. But suppressing or denying our feelings prevents change; we remain 'stuck' and rigid. Unexpressed emotions never disappear of their own accord. We may try to put them behind us, but eventually this will only lead to more problems. Repressed emotions often express themselves physically. Many illnesses have an emotional component that has become locked within the body. Physical pain can be just another form of emotional expression that we are not acknowledging.

In our attempts to escape emotional pain, we shut out the feelings that make living such a wonderful experience – the ability to love and feel loved, spontaneity and creativity suffer as a consequence. We lose the opportunity to know ourselves and discover the unique qualities that make us who we are, giving way to a dry and monotonous existence that lacks any meaning.

Sometimes we feel emotions that are scary and overwhelming. When this happens we try anything we can to avoid facing them. Once an emotion becomes stuck, it ceases to hold any purpose other than to keep a person frozen in time. At worst this can be totally devastating, especially after an intense trauma, and the person becomes trapped within the experience, unable to move forward.

Many of us do not have to contend with this level of emotional distress, but at some time in our lives most of us will come across an emotional stumbling block that we find difficult to overcome. Perhaps we are held back by our own fear, consumed with anger or locked into resentment and blame, or plagued with feelings of low self-esteem, intense grief or a sense of guilt. None of us are immune to any of these feelings.

It is these emotions that The Emotional Freedom Technique addresses. The purpose of this book is to introduce you to a technique that will enhance your life. We invite you to discover for yourself the versatility and freedom that EFT can offer you.

# Introduction

There is a subtle transformation occurring within the field of medicine and emotional healing. Alternative therapies and the theories that support them are attracting widespread interest and research as public demand increases. This has led to the introduction of new and exciting methods that complement the current models of healing. Alternative approaches are gathering momentum. A new awareness is growing that aspires to a more natural and non-invasive approach to healing the body and the mind.

Medical science has made enormous progress in the treatment of disease and life threatening illness. Yet, for all the technology and scientific research, it lacks a basic understanding of the true essence of an individual as a whole. How our thoughts, feelings, beliefs and attitudes influence our health has been largely ignored. However, within a holistic framework, the relationship between the mind, body and spirit is seen as fundamental in the role of producing health.

Many people are now familiar with the concept that the body can be healed through the mind, yet few people realize that you can also heal the mind through the body. At the cutting edge of this new paradigm is a technique known as The Emotional Freedom Technique (EFT) – a form of Energy Psychology that shares the same principles as the ancient art of acupuncture, which recognizes the existence of an inherent energy factor within all of us that is responsible for our overall health. This is the electrical/energetic blueprint of the body known as the meridian system.

The meridians are energetic pathways within the body that relay information to the entire system, as well as channelling vital energy to the organs and tissues of the physical body. It has been acknowledged that blockages within the meridian system can cause internal disruption and eventually lead to the onset of illness and disease.

Perhaps more subtle and less known is that the energy within each meridian also registers emotions, feelings and sensations. Every time we experience an emotion the body's energy system is influenced to a certain degree. The meridian system and our psychology are intricately linked. Acknowledging this, EFT has been designed to directly interact with the energy system, rebalancing and stabilizing the disruption that occurs when a distressing emotion is experienced. This enables our energies to flow freely again, leaving us relaxed and at peace.

An EFT session involves gently tapping a sequence of meridian points on the body, with the fingertips. This simple yet powerful technique re-balances the energies of the body, releasing unwanted emotions, allowing an inner sense of calm to return. Perhaps one of the most miraculous effects of this treatment is the speed with which emotional distress can be resolved – sometimes in little more than minutes – creating freedom from emotional problems or issues that may have troubled you for years. In itself, EFT appears to hold the answer to many modern day emotional difficulties such as stress, phobias, insecurities, and depression.

To some extent each and every one of us is held back by our emotional responses, either through an inability to express our true feelings, or through emotional reactions we have little control over. Attaining freedom from unwanted emotions is the desire of all of us. To be able to quickly release fears, worries and negative emotions is an incredible ability.

EFT can be applied in any circumstance regardless of the emotion or situation. This is because we all have 'feelings' or reactions to every problem that affects us, regardless of whether it is a work-related problem, financial worries, an issue of self-esteem or the frustrations of dealing with a difficult teenager. EFT can address all situations that provoke an emotional reaction or contain an emotional component. In fact, EFT can be used to treat problems from the past as well as the present and future.

Past events, such as severe shocks or intense feelings of grief that still have an influence upon us, can be released. Future events that provoke anxious anticipation – job interviews or plane journeys, for example – can be resolved. Many people have also gained relief and experienced dramatic changes when applying EFT to physical ailments such as jet lag, tension, addictive cravings, as well as a wide range of physical disorders.

Part I of *Emotional Healing in Minutes* looks at the historical development of the Emotional Freedom Technique, and the theory behind it, discovering the wide range of applications that EFT can offer.

Part II will guide you step-by-step through the technique itself, enabling you to use it as a self-help approach to resolving many of the emotional and physical problems you may encounter in life.

Part III contains strategies to deal with a host of specific problems, from Phobias, Beliefs and Addictions, Physical complaints and Weight Loss, to issues connected with Relationships. Often people will wish to visit an EFT practitioner.

Finally, Part IV gives you the information you need to find the right practitioner and what to expect when you get there. Also contained in this section are invaluable trouble-shooting tips for those learning to use the technique.

The current applications of EFT have barely scratched the surface of future possibilities. It is a simple, safe and extremely powerful technique that enables every individual to access his or her own inner healing ability. Adults and children alike can benefit. EFT can be applied via a therapist (when dealing with deep trauma) or used for personal self-help. It is very easy to learn and, once grasped, it should take no more than a few minutes to carry out, wherever you are, offering you complete freedom at your fingertips. It really is a remarkable self-help approach that offers an entirely new way in which to resolve emotional distress and attain rapid relief from all manner of psychological limitations. We wish you every success and happiness.

# part 1

# Introducing Emotional Healing

## Chapter 1

# The Story of EFT

There are many valuable therapeutic approaches being re-discovered today that all have one thing in common, namely a recognition of an energetic component responsible for optimum health and well-being. Energy therapies are on the increase, offering new and alternative ways in which to achieve emotional harmony and physical health. The diverse range of energy therapies currently available includes:

| | |
|---|---|
| Acupressure | Reflexology |
| Acupuncture | Reiki (and other forms of hands-on healing) |
| Cranio-sacral Therapy | Shiatsu |
| Flower Essences | Tai Chi |
| Homeopathy | Traditional Chinese Medicine |
| Kinesiology | Yoga |
| Metamorphic Technique | |

One of the main qualities that energy therapies possess is the ability to address the psychological as well as the physical aspects of a person, enabling positive changes within the thoughts, attitudes and feelings of an individual. For this reason energy therapies can achieve much more than just symptom management.

Although each particular system has its own characteristics, there are common threads that link each and every one. Together, they acknowledge that the energies of the body are vital to attaining health and well-being. The treatment is focused at the energetic level and by releasing disturbances within the energy system, physical and emotional imbalances can be corrected.

If we maintain a healthy and harmonious energy system, physical health and emotional well-being are easily achieved. When out of balance, disorder and disruption are likely to occur. EFT has drawn upon the knowledge of the body's energy system and taken it one step further, by devising a way to intervene directly with the disruption caused by distressing thoughts and feelings. EFT focuses directly on our negative responses and works quickly to neutralize the discomfort, bringing rapid relief.

# A BRIEF
## HISTORY
# OF EFT

EFT was developed by American engineer Gary Craig. He had a life-long interest in helping other people overcome their emotional limitations and devoted much of his time to investigating various psychological treatments of one form or another. For many years he worked with Neuro-Linguistic Programming (NLP), until he discovered a revolutionary technique developed by clinical psychologist Dr Roger Callahan Ph.D.

Roger Callahan had devised a complete system of psychological healing, based on the meridians, known as Thought Field Therapy (TFT). It was a completely natural and non-invasive technique which has the capacity to eliminate negative emotions, beliefs and traumatic memories rapidly and often permanently. The inspiration for his method came from Acupuncture combined with the modern day practice of Kinesiology.

In his capacity as a clinical psychologist, Callahan had been treating a client, Mary, for over a year and a half. The following story describes how Callahan happened on TFT.

### mary's story – phobia of water

For as long as Mary could remember she had suffered from an intense phobia of water. This included rain, puddles and even seeing water on television! She could only tolerate bathing in a few centimetres of water and could not leave her house if it was raining. Large bodies of water such as the sea terrified her. Since childhood, Mary had also experienced horrendous nightmares about water and her life was a misery. No one within her family knew how this phobia had developed or if there had been any form of trigger.

In an attempt to alleviate her suffering, Roger Callahan tried every form of conventional psychotherapy known to him, including desensitization and hypnotherapy. Marginal progress had been made and she could now sit by his swimming pool during their sessions, as long as she didn't look at the water.

One particular afternoon she described 'an awful feeling in her stomach' which occurred whenever she even thought about water. Desperate to help, and feeling that he had nothing to lose, he suggested that she tapped under her eye. Callahan knew that according to the meridian map of the body, the stomach meridian began just below the eye. No one could have predicted what happened next. Not only did Mary lose the awful feeling in her stomach, but also her fear of water completely vanished and within an instant her life-long phobia had disappeared. Mary immediately rushed over to the swimming pool and started splashing her face with water. Callahan was startled as he watched Mary move towards the deep end of the swimming pool. Anxious, because he knew she could not swim, he shouted to her to be careful. Mary, filled with delight, replied that although her fear had miraculously vanished she had not lost her reason; she knew she could not swim. Mary's phobia and nightmares have never returned.

Callahan went on to develop his discovery and nearly two decades later the method has been refined to incorporate tapping points on the body relating to all the major meridians, thus enabling all manner of psychological problems and limitations to be addressed. He established certain 'tapping' points that related to specific problems and discovered precise sequences that needed to be performed.

Callahan identified precise tapping combinations for a wide range of problems, including such conditions as anxiety, addictions and phobias. He also created a system of diagnosis that indicated which particular meridians needed to be addressed within each individual and the correct order in which they needed to be treated. Callahan went on to author several books including *The Five Minute Phobia Cure*, *Why You Eat When You're Not Hungry* and *The Rapid Treatment of Panic, Agoraphobia and Anxiety*.

Gary Craig trained under Callahan and became proficient in using TFT. He went on to develop a system of his own – The Emotional Freedom Technique – which he felt simplified the process and made it easily accessible to everyone to use and apply. Knowing that each meridian was interlinked with the others in a continuing energy loop meant that by removing a blockage from one meridian, the entire circuit would automatically clear. He felt that there was no longer any need to locate which specific meridians were disrupted or their precise treatment order. Additionally, as there were only 14 points in total, Craig suggested that if they were all used, the same results could be produced as well as giving the entire energy system a complete overhaul at the same time. He produced a revised treatment plan that could be used for all problems – physical, emotional and psychological. It was easy to learn and perform and, in his opinion, it was just as effective.

Gary Craig teamed up with Adrienne Fowlie to develop EFT further and was invited to put his system to the test. The opportunity arose to work with traumatized Vietnam Veterans. This is what Gary has to say about that experience:

> 'They had Post Traumatic Stress Disorder (PTSD) which is among the most severe form of emotional disorders known. Every day these men relive the catastrophes of war ... like being forced to shoot innocent civilians (including young children) ... burying people in trenches ... and watching their own dear friends die or be dismembered. The sounds of gunfire, bombs and screams ricochet in their heads day and night. Sometimes only drugs ease the ever-present aches of war.

> 'They sweat. They cry. They have headaches and anxiety attacks. They are depressed and in pain. They have fears and phobias and are afraid to go to sleep at night because of their nightmares. Many have been in therapy for 20 years ... with very little relief.

> 'I still remember how thrilled I was when the Veterans Administration invited Adrienne and me to bring EFT to our soldiers. They gave us free rein to counsel with these men in any way we wanted. This would be the ultimate test regarding the power of EFT. If all it did was make a modest, but noticeable,

difference in the lives of these severely disabled men, most people would have considered it successful. In fact, it did much more. One of the video cases was about Rich, who had been in therapy for 17 years for his PTSD. He had:

- Over 100 haunting war memories, many of which he relived daily.
- A major height phobia, aggravated by having made over 50 parachute jumps.
- Insomnia – it took him three or four hours to get to sleep every night, even under quite strong medication.

'After using EFT with him, every trace of those problems vanished. Like most people, Rich had a hard time believing that those rather strange-seeming procedures would work. But he was willing to give them a try. We started with his height phobia and after about 15 minutes with EFT it had gone. He tested it by going several storeys up in a building and looking down over a fire escape. To his amazement, he had no phobic reaction whatsoever. We then applied EFT to several of his most intense war memories and neutralized all of them within an hour. He still remembers them, of course, but they no longer have any emotional charge. We taught the techniques to Rich so he could work on the rest of his war memories by himself. Within a few days they were all neutralized. They no longer bothered him. As a result, his insomnia went away. Two months later I spoke with Rich on the phone. He was still free of the problems. That's real emotional freedom. It's the end of years of torment. It's like walking out of a prison. And I had the privilege of handing him the keys! This is the promise of EFT.'

**Chapter 2**

# EFT – How It Works

'The cause of all negative emotions is a disruption in the body's energy system'
Gary Craig

## THE MERIDIANS

The meridian system is an intricate web of energy pathways that flow through the body. These pathways closely resemble the nervous system and they are responsible for channelling energy through the physical body.

Traditional Chinese Medicine maintains that physical vitality and peace of mind are reliant upon the clear and even flow of these invisible energies. If disturbed, disease or emotional problems may result. Therapies such as Acupuncture and Acupressure directly stimulate, balance or unblock the meridian channels to relieve physical illness and promote psychological health.

There are 14 major meridians that form an interconnected circuit – 12 of these pass through the main organs of the body. Identical sets of meridians are found on each side of the body. The two remaining meridians control and modify the supply of energy within the entire circuit.

The two end points of each meridian channel appear close to the surface of the skin. Spaced along each meridian there are key points, which act as amplifiers or gateways. These are commonly known as acupuncture or acupressure points. EFT uses the end points of each meridian.

# ENERGETIC DISRUPTION

EFT views our emotional reactions as the direct result of disturbances within the energy system. The first indication of an emotion is a change in the body's energetic or electrical state. Conventional methods focus on treating distressing memories or thought processes that cause us emotional pain. Roger Callahan discovered that an additional stage occurs between accessing a painful memory and the resulting negative emotion. This is that traumatic memories and thoughts cause an energetic disturbance within the body (Fig. 1). This disturbance is then experienced as a negative emotion. Once the energetic disruption is released, memories cease to hold the original emotional intensity, enabling negative feelings to be resolved quickly. This extra dimension is the vital link within emotional healing. In essence, the energy system holds the key to unlocking your troubling emotions.

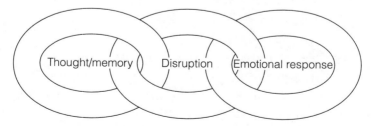

*Figure 1 – The Chain Reaction*

When our energies are flowing smoothly we feel calm and peaceful. When the energy system is disturbed we become out of balance and emotional. Blockages within the body's energy can lead to all manner of negative reactions and experiences. Energetic disturbances can limit your functioning, creativity and potential. They can be likened to boulders in a stream creating a blockage within the channel, preventing a free flow of energy around the body. Removing the boulders allows balance and equilibrium to return. Energetic disruption can be caused by any stimulus that triggers a painful memory or upsetting thought. For instance:

- **Sounds** – the tone of someone's voice, accents, a piece of music, emergency sirens, machinery, explosive noises, the dentist's drill, a child screaming.
- **Smells** – someone's favourite perfume, the fragrance of certain flowers, tobacco smoke, disinfectant and anaesthetic smells, vomit, foods, alcohol on the breath.
- **Sights** – colours, a person who resembles someone from the past, a film on television, blood, syringes, the sea, uniforms, violence, scenes of war, broken glass.
- **Objects** – jewellery, electronic appliances, mementos, weapons, gas masks, clothing.
- **Environments** – thunder, poor driving conditions, boat trips, places that remind us of a trauma, lifts and confined spaces, darkness, wide-open spaces, heights, tunnels, flying.
- **Animals** – insects, bees, wasps, spiders, worms, frogs, dogs, jellyfish, snakes, bats, birds, cats, rodents, reptiles, horses, cows, maggots.

- **Trigger Words** – language that holds certain associations, such as, *'No!', 'Shut up!', 'You're stupid, ugly, fat', 'Four eyes', 'Sissy', 'It's all your fault'.*

# EXERCISE – PERSONAL TRIGGERS

Identify any triggers that provoke a reaction for you. Write them down and keep the list to be used later when you start applying EFT.

# THOUGHT PATTERNS

The body and brain function on an electro-chemical level, so our thoughts are constantly creating patterns of electrical energy. In turn, neurotransmitters, hormones and chemicals are released in response to this electrical energy. By interrupting this chain of events the predetermined emotional reaction can be altered.

# EXERCISE – THOUGHT ENERGY

The effect of our thoughts can be demonstrated quite clearly. Spend a few minutes thinking about an unhappy or negative memory in your past. As soon as you begin to remember this event, something very tangible should happen to your energy. How do you feel?

Now repeat the same process, this time thinking about a positive event. If you cannot think of a happy time in your life, focus your thoughts on the positive things that you would *like* to happen in the future. Do you feel quite different to the first attempt?

Positive thoughts invariably produce a more energizing and vibrant feeling than negative thoughts. These subtle changes within our electrical energy affect our attitude, emotional responses and physical bodies. A single negative thought can influence your mood for anything from a few minutes to several hours.

In this modern age where people are constantly thinking about their mortgage, their performance at work or relationship problems, negative thinking can multiply exponentially, causing a bombardment of relentless thoughts and concerns that eventually overwhelms the energy system. If left unchecked this can lead to depression, as the energy field becomes weighed down by our 'heavy' responsibilities.

By correcting disrupted energy flow, EFT effectively breaks the link between thoughts and negative emotions, leaving all memories intact, but releasing the emotional intensity connected with them. Once the emotional charge is removed from a traumatic incident or future event, the negative emotions associated with it can no longer be felt.

### kirsty's story – car accident memory

Kirsty was involved in a car accident many years ago. Since that time, she had felt anxious and out of control whenever she was a passenger in a car. After one EFT session during

emotional healing

which she tapped for the distressing memory, she was able to talk about the accident in a calm and relaxed manner. She realized that although she could remember everything that had happened, her fear had gone. The thought of the incident and the possibility of being a passenger in the future failed to produce an emotional response. Kirsty was pleased to discover that she could now travel quite happily as a passenger without the anxious feelings that used to haunt her.

# ENERGETIC PATTERNS

The energy that flows through our body is unlike our physical energy – it is our own consciousness. Our energy is an integral part of our make-up. It forms an energetic replica of our physical and emotional being and is a balancing and regulating factor for the entire system.

Repetitive emotional reactions can be seen as an energetic pattern that becomes imprinted on our psyche, causing us to react in a similar way repeatedly. This may explain why so many people become stuck in certain emotional responses or modes of behaviour.

Phobias, fears and anxieties are good examples of this. Phobias can be likened to a 'stuck record' response that continually repeats itself. Rationally we know that a spider across the other side of the room will not harm us. Statistically, the chances of us being in an aeroplane crash are relatively small. We realize most of our fears are irrational, unfounded or unlikely to happen, yet the emotional intensity is just as strong.

Such patterns can be found throughout our personal lives. There are many recurring themes that appear within families and relationships, such as feelings of hurt, anger, abandonment or betrayal. These themes often reach far back into our personal history and may have been imprinted on us during childhood or occur as a direct result of an earlier experience. Liberating ourselves from these ingrained patterns has been made easier through using the EFT process. Roger Callahan referred to this as 'breaking nature's code'.

# BREAKING THE VICIOUS CIRCLE

Meridian therapies have a way of neutralizing the energetic disruption within the body and returning it back to normal. By gently 'tapping' certain emotional release points on the body, the disrupted energy and emotional charge connected with a traumatic event is removed. Through making an energetic adjustment in such a way, you can alter the upsetting emotions that surface after distressing events. As a result, the energetic template is broken, allowing resolution of the original emotional state. This then liberates you from the emotional hold a situation or difficulty has had.

# EXERCISE – EXPERIENCING YOUR OWN ENERGY FIELD

This exercise will help you to experience your own energy field. There are many different ways in which to do this. The example below is a good place to start:

1 Make sure you are sitting comfortably.

2 Relax and clear your mind, this is an exercise in feeling not thinking. It is important not to try too hard, just be receptive and let it happen.

3 Gently rub the palms of your hands together a couple of times.

4 In slow motion, gradually pull your hands apart approximately half a centimetre. For the best results keep your fingers closed.

5 Then slowly bring your hands together again, without allowing them to physically touch each other.

6 Repeat this process, slowly moving back and forwards, slightly further each time, until you work up to being roughly 15cm apart. (Remember not to let your hands touch.)

7 You should now feel an 'energetic pull' between your hands. This is experienced in different ways, but can be described as a feeling of static, friction, heat, tingling, or as a magnetic pull.

8 You may wish to bring your hands up to your face or move them gently around the body to experience the energy that surrounds you.

Experiment in finding a way that suits you. It may be easier to feel a friend's energy first. Some people can actually see the energy surrounding people, so don't be alarmed if you catch glimmers of light or colour while you practise this exercise.

**Chapter 3**

# The Friendly Therapy

## THE ADVANTAGES OF EFT

There are so many advantages that EFT has to offer, not least of which is a genuine freedom from your deepest fears and lifelong limitations. EFT has at least an 85% success rate, which means there is a good chance that it will work for you. Most people experience significant, if not a total, release from their problems. An idea of the wide range of problems that can be addressed with EFT will be given later in this chapter. First, we'll look at some of the unique benefits that can be derived from the therapy.

### Relieving Pain, Not Reliving It

With most forms of counselling or psychotherapy, we are expected to relive the turn of events that has led us to our present state. In EFT, when the energy system is re-balanced, emotional shifts occur rapidly. All the usual stages of emotional healing are visited – they are just accessed much quicker. Lasting results are achieved in minutes, rather than months or, in some cases, years of therapy, so you don't have to relive all your former painful experiences!

The therapy process should not be more traumatic than the original incident! Identifying the feelings or upsetting thoughts involved is all that is required in order to eliminate their negative effects. As soon as a feeling surfaces it is quickly neutralized. This technique does not teach you how to cope with your difficulty or to find strategies to manage your distress. It is designed to remove the emotional charge that keeps you locked into the problem. This makes healing through EFT gentle and relatively pain free.

## Healing the Emotions

EFT can be applied to a broad spectrum of emotional difficulties, from niggling irritations through to fundamental core issues. The technique does not alter and it is exactly the same for all conditions. The process works as effectively for deep-seated suffering as it does for everyday problems, as was demonstrated in the case of Terry.

### terry's story – parent issues

'My father died 12 years ago, but I did not grieve or mourn. I felt no sorrow or loss because I felt I had lost my 'real' father some 18 years before. His passing was something that I accepted would happen one day and I attended the funeral only at the request of my mother. Since his death I had spoken of him less and less, because my memories of him were all negative. It gave me no pleasure to recall them. My mother recognized my anger so did not mention her husband, who she greatly missed.

'In recent years I had questioned whether my feelings towards my father were misplaced. It wasn't until finding out about EFT that the prospect of addressing these issues came to the fore. The session was quite emotional for me, as I struggled with the emotions surrounding this unloved – dare I say, hated –

parent of mine. Then, suddenly, it was all over and I felt as if a weight had been lifted from me. My world seemed a little lighter and more loving than before. I felt sorry for the man who I had despised and hated. I wished I had shown more compassion when he was alive, especially towards the end of his life. For the first time in years I could speak about my father to my friends and especially my mother who, despite his shortcomings, loved him dearly. Her joy alone made the effort worthwhile, because knowing of my feelings, she had never spoken of him, although she had desperately wanted and needed to.'

## Lasting Relief

The changes and transformations that occur through applying this technique are yours to keep! Once every aspect of the problem has been addressed, the results are often permanent. People report that their problems lose all intensity after only a few minutes of treatment. Issues that have caused intense distress in the past, sometimes over long periods of time, pale into insignificance. Events in the future that would usually produce a high degree of stress become easy to negotiate.

No matter how long-standing your suffering has been, clearing the energy system can release its effects. This is because emotions are timeless. All emotions are felt in the present, even when the event is yet to happen. Because of this, EFT can be applied to past memories that are still distressing, future events that produce anxiety and trepidation, as well as current emotional difficulties.

emotional healing

## The Simple Therapy

EFT is extremely simple to learn and apply. This means that, as well as working with a therapist, it can be used effectively for self-help. Everyone can learn the basics in less than half an hour. It is an uncomplicated and straightforward approach that even children find simple to apply. Once learnt, the technique remains the same whatever the issue. Because of its very simplicity, the potency and potential of EFT is often underestimated.

Sometimes our feelings derive from early childhood experiences, before we are able to communicate our needs. This can make it hard to pinpoint or verbalize the original cause of our pain. The source may also lie within the unconscious mind, beyond our conscious awareness. This can be very frustrating, as the reason behind our feelings can be elusive and difficult to explain. When using an energetic approach to healing, it is not essential to know where your feelings stem from, nor is it necessary to identify the incident that causes each emotion. The fact that they exist is enough to elicit a healing response.

## Rapid Healing

If the energetic disruption caused by turbulent emotions is removed, change can be easy, swift and painless. Once the residue of emotional energy has been cleared, we are able to reach a quick resolution of our original problem. We find it hard to accept that deep inner healing can take place so rapidly. Believing that change takes a long time to come about and only occurs after a lot of blood, sweat and tears. Yet we make changes every day; as soon as we change our mind about something our reality soon follows. Changing can really be that simple. Once the emotional attachment to a problem is cleared, a solution can be quickly found and radical adjustments can take place.

Quite often people feel that by rapidly losing an emotional response to a situation, they will automatically miss out on the lesson to be learnt. This is understandable, but if you have already experienced the emotions once, why do you want to again? EFT does not remove the 'gold' that exists within our emotional struggles. None of the 'lessons' or 'realizations' are lost during the process. Lessons continue to be learnt, insight into a problem is still gained and understanding is reached. The arrival is just quicker, more of an 'Aha!' experience than a drawn-out process.

## Expressing NOT Suppressing

Unlike using medication, EFT does not seek to suppress unwanted emotional reactions, but to release and resolve them. This technique is not about denying, repressing or disassociating from your feelings. This would be unhealthy and only leads to the creation of more problems. Unexpressed emotions can vent themselves in other ways, producing physical health problems or deeper emotional problems, such as depression. Denied emotions find other ways to express themselves, as neuroses, anxiety or obsessions.

To be emotionally healed of our past, it is necessary to access, assimilate and resolve our original emotional issues. Often, this process occurs naturally over time. However, some people find it impossible to overcome their anguish and, as a result, remain trapped in emotional pain. EFT enables true healing to take place, allowing a person to pass through all the vital healing stages.

## Holistic Healing

The energy that circulates through us all is connected to every aspect of our being. Each time you apply EFT, not only do you rid yourself of problems,

emotional healing

you also give your energy system a complete overhaul, improving your general health, happiness and well-being. Because EFT uses your own energy system to create changes, the treatment is tailor-made for you as an individual. What one person needs to accomplish from healing will differ from the next. Whatever you need to resolve will be stored in *your* energy system.

In keeping with holistic principles, EFT focuses on the root cause of an emotional issue as well as the symptoms of distress. Frequently, it will uncover the deeper origins of fears, phobias and addictive cravings. Wendy's case illustrates how the underlying reasons for a problem can be discovered through EFT. Wendy had a severe phobia of cotton wool, but she had no idea where it stemmed from. While receiving treatment, a traumatic memory from her childhood was revealed. Here is her story:

### wendy's story – cotton wool phobia

'Ever since I can remember, I have had an intense aversion to cotton wool. Even the words "cotton wool" were unpleasant to me. The feel of the stuff, the touch of it, even the sound of it being pulled apart set my nerves jangling and on edge.

'As I addressed the issue with EFT, my thoughts went back to my first childhood stay in hospital, for a tonsillectomy, when I was two and a half. It was a horrific experience for me – I was left all alone, full of grief for three days without seeing my mum. I felt deserted and cried continuously. I remember cotton wool swabs being used daily to clean my wounds. This experience left me with a dreadful stutter which took a year or more to disappear. And this was where my problems with cotton wool began.

'Before the treatment, I couldn't bear to hold cotton wool and would back off if anyone approached me with it. After the session I sat for a couple of hours holding a lump of the stuff with no problems at all. So EFT worked for me. It is strange how something as inoffensive as cotton wool could be the focus of all my bad experiences, trauma and frightened emotions.'

# THE APPLICATIONS OF EFT

As practitioners, it took us a long time to fully appreciate the scope and far-reaching effects of re-aligning the energy system. The scope of EFT applications is as broad as the most fertile imagination. The versatility is amazing. Some of the most common uses of EFT include:

| | |
|---|---|
| addictions | low self esteem |
| agoraphobia | migraines |
| anger | nightmares |
| anxiety | obsessions |
| bitterness | pain management |
| claustrophobia | panic attacks |
| compulsions | phobias |
| depression | physical aches and pains |
| fears | post-traumatic stress |
| grief | resentment |
| guilt | sadness |
| habits | shame |
| insomnia | slimming |
| limiting beliefs | sports performance |

stopping smoking                    traumatic memories

stress

It is not essential to have a 'problem' to benefit from this technique. The method works exceedingly well for issues that never reach a therapist's office, issues that in some way you have just learnt to live with. EFT can be incorporated into your daily life and applied to minor irritations, restrictions, limitations or any other area, as and when needed.

## Work-related Issues

The workplace can produce all manner of stresses and EFT can help to ease the ever-present irritations, frustrations and challenges, whether in relation to your boss, colleagues, deadlines or learning new skills. The technique can be used to release pent up energy and feelings of pressure, or applied whenever you feel tired or lethargic.

One work-related area for which people often apply EFT is a fear of public speaking. People with this phobia can suffer a tremendous amount of stress leading up to talking in public. Fears of forgetting words, making a fool of yourself or painful shyness can all be eradicated by simply tapping the meridian points. EFT can effectively remove blocks to success and personal performance – use it before meetings, presentations, cold calls or any situation where you feel under pressure to achieve. A young woman called Shelley used EFT to promote confidence and assertiveness within her job.

### shelley's story – self-confidence at work
Shelley had started a job as sales assistant in a clothes store. She was relieved about this as it was only a few weeks before Christmas and she needed the extra money. Just a few days

later she was told that she would not be paid until after Christmas as the wages were only paid once a month.

She was extremely upset and angry that she would not be able to afford Christmas presents for her family. We tapped for her anger, frustration and upset and she felt a little better. We then suggested that maybe she could ask for an advance and this was when deeper issues surfaced. She didn't feel 'good enough' to ask for the money. She also felt that the manager-ess didn't like her. We tapped for *'I believe the manageress doesn't like me'*, *'I don't believe they will let me have a sub'* and *'I don't feel confident enough to ask'*.

After the session Shelley felt totally different. Her energy had lifted and she felt good about herself. The next day she asked if she could have an advance. The manageress smiled and said 'Of course, I'll phone head office right away.' She also praised Shelley on the standard of her work. A few weeks later she was asked if she would like to train for a managerial position.

## Aggravations and Irritations

No matter how laid back we are, it can still be easy to lose our temper when under pressure. The old saying of 'count to ten' can be replaced by 'tap for it'. A few minutes of tapping should be enough to release the tension. Partners' annoying habits, screaming children, traffic jams, interfering parents can all be soothed away quickly.

### pam's story – irritation

Pam had an adorable little dog called Lucy. However, Lucy had a very excitable nature and car journeys with her were an ordeal. She would squeal the entire time. This behaviour caused Pam to dread taking Lucy anywhere in the car. She had tried everything she could think of to break the habit, but to no avail. After learning about EFT, she decided to give it a try. Pam and her husband set off in the car to take Lucy for a walk and, true to form, Lucy began her horrendous noise. Immediately, Pam began tapping for all the different elements that annoyed her. She tapped for:

> 'Her barking drives me mad.'
> 'I can't stand the noise Lucy makes.'
> 'I want to throw her out of the window.'
> 'This ceaseless barking!'

While tapping, the irritation began to subside and Pam realized that she was relaxed and enjoying the view from the window. Lucy's barking no longer troubled her but her poor husband was getting very uptight. They agreed that next time Pam would drive so that her husband could tap away his annoyances.

Physical irritations such as bites, bumps and stings can also be relieved by this method, as well as aggravations such as hiccups and sneezing fits.

## Sports Performance

Most sports require a focused and positive frame of mind to ensure success. How you feel on a particular day often reflects your overall performance. Performance levels can be improved by using EFT. Some benefits include:

- Removing the nerves before an important match, game or competition
- Enhancing technique when a particular block or challenge exists
- Diffusing negative memories of failures or disappointments
- Building the confidence to achieve high standards
- Increasing motivation and stamina

## Self-image

How many of us are completely happy with the way we look? Most people feel discontented with some aspect of their appearance; they are *'too fat'*, *'too thin'*, *'too short'* or *'too tall'*. Or they may feel ugly or unattractive because of one particular part of their body – *'My nose is too big'*, *'I don't like my thighs'*, *'I wish my teeth didn't stick out'*, *'If only my bum wasn't so big'*. These insecurities can erode our self-esteem. In the same way, some people feel *'clumsy'*, *'awkward'* or *'dumb'* and this can prevent them from enjoying certain activities. For some, reassurance alone is not enough to allay these doubts and insecurities but EFT will help you to overcome negative thoughts and feelings connected with your self-image.

Feeling uncomfortable about ourselves can lead to shyness, blushing, stammering or profuse sweating and these can all cause acute embarrassment. It is very easy to find ourselves caught in a vicious cycle, becoming tense at the mere thought that we might blush or trip over our words, thus compounding the fear of it happening again. EFT can help break the chain of events that precede such complaints.

## Self-imposed Limitations

In the same way that poor self-image can make us unhappy and insecure, negative beliefs about ourselves can lead to self-imposed limitations. *'I can't ...'*, *'I'm no good at ...'*, *'I've never been good at that'*. These negative beliefs hold us back in many ways. They stop us from attempting new things and keep us trapped within the apparent safety of our personal comfort zone. Unfortunately, the limitations we put on ourselves prevent us from doing things that could improve and expand our lives. Before you turn down an opportunity because of fear, or because you believe *'I could never do that'*, target the negative emotion with EFT and watch what happens!

## Decision-making

Have you ever made a decision based on an emotion only to regret it at a later date? When making a personal decision, we are often influenced by outside influences. How will others react? What will they say? Am I being selfish? Then there is the need for parental approval or fear of being judged. All these conflicting energies can disrupt our train of thought and make decision-making very confusing. Next time an important decision needs to be made, try using EFT to neutralize the fear, self-doubt or conflicting emotions that prevent you from making an informed and centred choice.

## Confronting Life's Problems

The application of this subtle energy therapy can be used in so many circumstances that it truly is a companion for life. The breadth of possibilities where EFT can help is demonstrated by Sue's story.

## sue's story – unhappiness

'I stumbled across EFT at a point in my life when I felt that a
lot of changes were needed in order for me to be happy. I kept
finding myself falling in love with the wrong type of person and
choosing totally inappropriate jobs. I got to the point of being
bitter and resentful. I thought it must be everyone else's fault
– certainly not mine.

'The angels must have had pity on me when I heard about
EFT. After all, it was painless (no needles), did not take long (I
had limited time being a working mother) and it did not cost
the earth. It sounded too good to be true, but I felt that I had
nothing to lose.

'The first feeling that surfaced was anger – I did not feel comfortable with anger at the best of times. In fact, I was more
afraid of other people's anger than of my own. I followed the
simple procedure that starts with the recognition of a negative
emotion, tapping all the points and within two minutes it was all
over. I didn't know why, but when I tuned in again, I burst out
laughing. The relief and release of tension was incredible. I
became excited and confident and wanted to try it on lots of
other things. I used it for simple things like headaches,
stomach upsets, backache, PMT. I then went on to more
complex issues like fear of deep water, fear of aggression, fear
of rejection, being alone, not having enough money. Each time,
there was an immediate effect – once, a pain in my shoulder
that I had experienced for many years, literally shifted down
along my arm and disappeared while tapping.

'One aspect central to my original problem was the feeling that other people were responsible for my happiness, or the lack of it. EFT made it easy for me to see the connection between my early experiences and my adult choices. My experience of EFT has freed me of countless negative beliefs and emotions. I lead a different life now – one with very little fear. I am confident and face new challenges every day. I can finally look for the things that I want to be doing, instead of staying in situations because of fear. If fear comes up or I feel unable to cope, I have a quick session of EFT.'

If you are grappling with a certain area of your life, or feel stuck in a rut, use EFT to work through your feelings of frustration. Whether you are caught in an unrewarding career, an unproductive relationship or unfulfilling circumstances, balancing the meridians will break up the stagnant energy and layers of resistance to making positive changes. No matter what the area of difficulty, this technique will help you to get the energy flowing back into your life again.

# part 2

# The Emotional Freedom Technique

register a disruption within the energy system. Saying *'I am anxious and afraid of giving this speech'* generates a stronger emotional charge than *'I want to be calm and relaxed'*.

Naming the problem you are currently experiencing will produce better results than a statement based in the past or that does not hold true. As you think about your problem, ask yourself how it makes you feel in this present moment.

### Formulating the Perfect Statement

- Be as specific as possible
- Use the present tense
- Describe how you feel right now, rather than what you are hoping to achieve

For instance:

'I feel angry.'

This statement would be a good place to start but it can still be improved. Take a few minutes to think about why you are angry. The most beneficial outcomes are achieved by creating a precise statement that would be more like:

'I feel angry that Bob wouldn't listen to me.'
'I feel angry that Bob let me down.'

Equally, if you are feeling hurt from a past action, form a sentence that best describes how you feel now:

'I feel hurt that I wasn't included.'
'I am hurt that I was left out.'

Physical problems also need formulating into a sentence. It is very important that you describe the *feeling* of pain or discomfort you are experiencing, rather than the name of your disorder. Use the language that you actually use when complaining of your condition:

'A *stabbing* pain behind the eyes'
'This *tight* band around my head'
'I have a *sick feeling* in my stomach'
'*Stiffness* in my neck'

Now place the words *'Even though I ...'* in front of your chosen statement, followed by *'... I deeply and completely accept myself.'* For instance:

'Even though I feel angry that Bob wouldn't listen to me I deeply and completely accept myself.'
'Even though I fear failure I deeply and completely accept myself.'
'Even though I have this anxious feeling I deeply and completely accept myself.'
'Even though I am frightened of flying I deeply and completely accept myself.'
'Even though I am afraid to speak out and say how I feel I deeply and completely accept myself.'
'Even though I have this deep sadness I deeply and completely accept myself.'
'Even though I am nervous about this interview I deeply and completely accept myself.'

'Even though I am terrified that I will make a fool of myself I deeply and completely accept myself.'
'Even though I have this hot stabbing pain in my back I deeply and completely accept myself.'
'Even though I have a knot in my stomach I deeply and completely accept myself.'
'Even though I feel totally confused I deeply and completely accept myself.'
'Even though I feel depressed I deeply and completely accept myself.'
'Even though I feel lonely I deeply and completely accept myself.'

There are a number of reasons why this form of affirmation is used. Firstly, it promotes acceptance of the problem and of yourself. Secondly, it overrides any part of you that does not want to change or that has a hidden agenda to keep you as you are. This is known as 'Psychological Reversal' and we will look at this in more depth later in Chapter 7.

At first you may find it difficult or uncomfortable to say *'I deeply and completely accept myself'*, but it is not necessary to believe the affirmation. Its function is to neutralize any reversal of energy flow throughout the meridians. All you need to do is to say it with conviction to achieve the desired result.

The statement is best said aloud if possible, the more emphatically the better, but in social gatherings you can say it silently to yourself.

# Step 3 – Score Chart

Now give your issue a score from one to ten relating to its intensity, ten being the highest intensity. This will enable you to check if your problem is resolving after the first round. This is a good way to record your progress and map the results you are achieving. A deeply ingrained phobia may be described as an intense 'ten out of ten' reaction. A mild irritation may only score a three or four. As you work with EFT, the level of emotional discomfort declines, ultimately falling to a very low number or total zero. There is a chart you can use to record your scores on page 65.

# Step 4 – Affirmation Link-up

To give more energy to the affirmation one of two procedures need to be performed. Experiment with both and choose which you prefer.

### 1 – Locating the Tender Point/s

Place both hands on your upper chest just below your collarbone. Focusing on your problem, find a tender or sore area in this location. Lymphatic congestion often occurs in this part of our body and by stimulating the lymph nodes you help clear the energy system. Gently rub the sore spots in a circular motion while repeating your affirmation aloud three times. If for any reason you cannot use this area, apply the karate chop procedure.

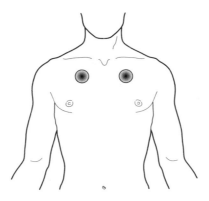

*Figure 2 – The Tender Points*

### 2 – Karate Chop Point

The karate chop points are located on the side of each hand, roughly an inch below the little finger. Gently tap either point with the fingertips for as long as it takes you to repeat your affirmation aloud three times.

*Figure 3 – The Karate Chop Point*

That concludes 'The Set-up'. Once memorized it should take a little under a minute to perform. Next, we go on to perform the tapping sequence.

# 2 THE SEQUENCE

This part of the EFT procedure is where the energetic disruption from the body is cleared. It begins with a 'Reminder Phrase' and then proceeds to clearing the energy circuit. Essentially, you will be tapping major meridian points chosen for their accessibility and ease of application.

## Step 5 – Reminder Phrase

A short reminder phase is used to keep your attention focused on the problem and to avoid distraction. It is said every time you tap a meridian point.

> 'This stabbing pain'
> 'This nervous feeling'
> 'This sadness'
> 'This fear of failure'
> 'This anger'
> 'This lonely feeling'

## Step 6 – Tapping Points

Using two fingers, gently tap each point in sequence approximately seven times, while repeating your reminder phase. Each point is below the next and this should make the sequence easier to remember. Take some time to familiarize yourself with the tapping positions. Each site is located on an acupressure point and may feel slightly more sensitive than the surrounding area. Trace your fingers through the routine until you feel totally confident with the order in which they appear.

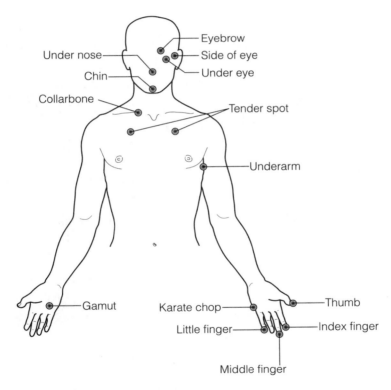

*Figure 4 – The EFT Tapping Positions*
Th = Thumb, IF = Index Finger, MF = Middle Finger, LF = Little Finger, KC = Karate Chop, The Gamut = Back of Hand, UA = Underarm

# TIPS ON
## TAPPING

You can tap with either hand on either side of the body and you can even switch halfway through if you like. Using two fingertips ensures that you locate the right vicinity. Tap firmly enough to propel energy through the meridian point, but not too hard to cause bruising. Each point is tapped approximately seven times, this can be as long as it takes you to breathe in and out, or say the reminder phrase three times.

| Meridian | EFT Tapping Point |
| --- | --- |
| Bladder | Beginning of Eyebrow (EB) |
| Gallbladder | Side of Eye (SE) |
| Stomach | Under Eye (UE) |
| Governing Vessel | Under the Nose (UN) |
| Conception Vessel | Chin (Ch) |
| Kidney | Collarbone (Cb) |
| Spleen | Underarm (Ua) |
| Lung | Thumb (Th) |
| Large Intestine | Index Finger (IF) |
| Circulation/Sex | Middle Finger (MF) |
| Heart | Little Finger (LF) |
| Small Intestine | Side of Hand (KC) |
| Triple Warmer | Back of Hand (Gamut) |
| Liver* | Under Breast (UB) |

*The liver point is not generally used within EFT due to social awkwardness.

*Figure 5 – The Major Meridians*

### Eyebrow (EB) – Bladder Meridian

Tap seven times at the beginning of your eyebrow point at the top of the nose, while repeating the reminder phrase.

### Side of Eye (SE) – Gallbladder Meridian

Tap seven times at the corner of the eye socket bone, while repeating the reminder phrase.

### Under the Eye (UE) – Stomach Meridian

Tap seven times at the centre of the bone below the eye, level with your pupil, while repeating the reminder phrase.

### Under the Nose (UN) – Governing Vessel

Tap the middle line between the nose and top lip seven times, while repeating the reminder phrase.

### Chin (Ch) – Central Vessel

Tap the middle of your chin, level with your gum line seven times, while repeating the reminder phrase.

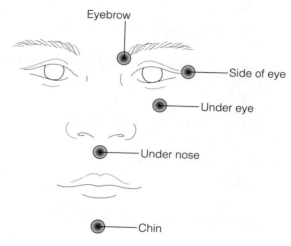

Figure 6 – Facial Positions

### Collarbone (Cb) – Kidney Meridian

Where the collarbone meets in the centre, just below the neck, a point can be found by moving down one inch and then outwards an inch, on either side. If you tap with all your fingers you will be assured of tapping the right spot. Tap this point seven times, while repeating the reminder phrase.

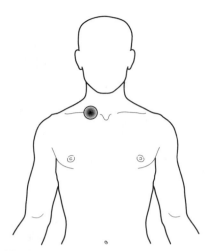

*Figure 7 – Collarbone Position*

## Underarm (Ua) – Spleen Meridian

On the torso under the arm, level with the nipple in men and the seam of a bra for women. Tap seven times, while repeating the reminder phrase.

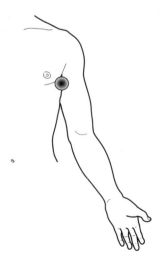

*Figure 8 – Underarm Position*

### Thumb (Th) – Lung Meridian

On the outside edge of the thumb, level with the base of your thumbnail. Tap this position seven times, while repeating the reminder phrase.

### Index Finger (IF) – Large Intestine Meridian

At the side edge of the index finger (nearest to thumb), level with the base of your fingernail you will find the index finger point. Tap here seven times, while repeating the reminder phrase.

### Middle Finger (MF) – Circulation/Sex Meridian

At the side of your middle finger (nearest to thumb), level with the base of the fingernail. Tap this place seven times, while repeating the reminder phrase.

### Little Finger (LF) – Heart Meridian

At the side of the little finger (nearest to thumb), level with the base of the fingernail. Tap seven times, while repeating the reminder phrase.

### Karate Chop (KC) – Small Intestine Meridian

On the side of each hand, roughly an inch below the little finger. Tap this point approximately seven times, while repeating the reminder phrase.

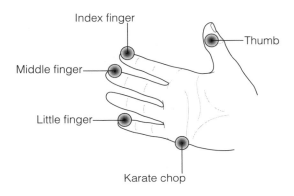

Index finger

Thumb

Middle finger

Little finger

Karate chop

*Figure 9 – Hand Positions*

Once you have completed this sequence, close your eyes and take a deep breath – in and then out.

# 3 THE GAMUT

## Step 7 – The Gamut

The Gamut Point can be found on the back of either hand, one centimetre below the knuckles between the ring and little finger.

*Figure 10 – Gamut Point*

Tap this point at the same time as performing the next few steps.

### Eye Movements

- Close your Eyes.
- Open your Eyes.
- While holding your head still look hard down right.
- While holding your head still look hard down left.
- While holding your head still look hard down right.
- While holding your head still look hard down left.
- Keeping your head perfectly still roll your eyes in an anti-clockwise direction.
- Repeat the same process rolling in a clockwise direction.
- Take a deep breath in and out. Allow a few moments for your energy to reconfigure.

These procedures may seem a little strange, but they do have an important function. We often process many of our feelings through our dreams. Rapid eye movement (REM) is the brain's way of clearing and sorting through many of the trials and tribulations that occur during waking hours. This can be observed during REM sleep. In moving the eyes in this exercise we recreate the brain's natural processing action. NLP creators, Richard Bandler and John Grinder, observed that we store different types of information in different areas of the brain. Our thoughts, memories, feelings, sensations, sounds and visual images all have their individual storage areas in the brain. These different mental functions can be accessed by means of certain eye positions. You may have noticed the particular eye movements people make when trying to remember a piece of information or when describing a physical sensation. Quite often people look in different directions when they are retrieving or tuning in to internal processes. Within EFT, rotating the eyes initiates a balancing action within the various parts of the brain. It also addresses and clears the different thoughts, memories and feelings that contribute to a problem.

# 4 THE SECOND SEQUENCE

## Step 8 – Second Sequence

Once you have completed the Gamut procedure, a second tapping sequence is repeated. Starting from the Eyebrow point, tap through to the Karate Chop point, repeating the reminder phrase as before.

## Step 9 – Reassessment

The first round of EFT is now complete. It is now time to check how you are feeling about your original problem. A good way to do this is to give it another score out of ten to see if there is any difference. You will often notice a significant change from your first level of intensity. For some people, one round of EFT is all that is required to be completely free of a problem. Their score for this issue would now register as zero. For others a few further rounds of adjustments may be needed.

## Step 10 – Round Adjustments

Depending on the depth of problem, the intensity level may drop by two or three. If your original feelings are slightly improved but still present, you will need to repeat the EFT round until the feeling resolves. This usually takes only a few rounds. When performing repeat round adjustments a slight alteration to your initial statement needs to be made. This informs the unconscious mind that you now wish to clear the *remaining* feelings that are connected to the problem, rather than the original feelings you had. Examples of this could be:

'Even thought I still feel anger I deeply and completely accept myself.'
'Even though I still feel frightened I deeply and com-pletely accept myself.'
'Even though my shoulder still hurts I deeply and completely accept myself.'
'Even though I still feel sad I deeply and completely accept myself.'

Then repeat the whole procedure from Step 1 to Step 9 again. Only this time use a reminder phrase that includes the word *remaining*. For instance:

> 'This remaining fear of spiders'
> 'This remaining guilt'
> 'This remaining height phobia'
> 'This remaining stiffness'

You may also find that a completely new 'Aspect' or feeling about the same problem surfaces; this is a very common occurrence. Usually when this happens you will need to switch your attention to the new element and address it with a complete EFT round (*see* Chapter 6).

Practise the different steps of the EFT Formula until you feel quite comfortable with the order of the routines. It can be learnt quite quickly and it should not take long to become proficient. Simply clear your mind and tap through the EFT points. This will give your energy system a general overhaul without focusing on a specific problem.

## THE TEN STEPS
## TO EFT

Step 1 – Identify the Problem

Step 2 – Formulate a Statement – The Set-up

Step 3 – Score Chart

Step 4 – Affirmation Link-up

Step 5 – Reminder Phrase

Step 6 – Tapping Points

emotional healing

Step 7 – The Gamut

Step 8 – The Second Sequence

Step 9 – Reassessment

Step 10 – Round Adjustments

## Chapter 5

# Energetic Shifts

Working with energy and consciousness enables deep levels of healing to take place very quickly. If the treatment is aimed at life enhancement and personal growth, vast change and transformation is possible. However, releasing unwanted energies can produce some novel sensations. As your energy system integrates these new changes and restructures itself, various things can happen. While these responses are only temporary, they are very significant.

Because we are all different, it is impossible to predict the exact sensations that you may experience, although there are some physical and emotional indications that regularly appear. These sensations are the body's natural response to an energetic shift. They illustrate in a very tangible way that the emotional energy connected to an issue is being discharged. If you observe any of the reactions mentioned below, you can be assured that a change has taken place.

# PHYSICAL
## INDICATIONS

### Sigh of Relief

As you work through the tapping positions you may feel inclined to sigh. You have probably observed how highly emotive situations, such as arguments, are often followed by sighs of relief once a satisfactory conclusion has been reached. Similarly, we often sigh to relieve tension. During a tapping session this process is mirrored. Emotional energy connected to the problem is literally expelled on the breath.

### Yawning

You may experience an overwhelming desire to yawn at certain stages throughout the treatment. On some occasions people report a series of intense yawns. Through yawning, deeply held energy is dissipated. This can be seen as a very positive sign that the treatment has taken effect and that pent-up energy is being released.

### Burping

This reaction is like trapped wind, only in this context it is trapped 'emotional wind' that is being cleared. It may be a little embarrassing but the results are extremely beneficial.

## Light-headedness

Some individuals describe light-headedness or a sensation of dizziness when using EFT. The energy that was originally tied-up in their issue is suddenly redirected, causing them to feel slightly strange for a few seconds. It is a brief reaction that reflects the adjustments occurring within the energy field and will only last momentarily.

## Sleepiness

A feeling of sleepiness may wash over you. Again this will not last and is similar to a feeling of relief after putting down a heavy load. It tends to happen when you finally let go of something at a deep level. It is a good indication and is seen as a healing reaction that occurs only as the body and mind completely relaxes.

Other physical sensations that may be experienced include: tingling, coldness, rushes of energy, heat, floating sensations, swaying and pins and needles.

# EMOTIONAL INDICATIONS

## Elation

You may not experience a physical sensation of energy clearance while using EFT, but the technique can produce a shift in your emotional state or outlook, such as feelings of elation. People often report that they suddenly feel more positive, happy and optimistic. It is interesting that feelings of 'lightness' can describe how it feels when a burden is lifted from your shoulders. Emotional problems can feel very heavy and we even use language that illustrates this:

*'Carrying emotional baggage', 'It weighs heavily on me', 'It weighs me down', 'It's such a burden'.* The sensation of lightness experienced after an EFT session results from heavy energies being removed from our energy field. People can also look lighter as if they have lost weight!

## Bewilderment

A familiar response to EFT is a form of momentary confusion. After working with your issue, you may become a little confused or unsure as to where the problem has gone. You may also have difficultly remembering the exact concern you were working on. This is natural and is a frequent event within energy therapies. Emotions can be neutralized so quickly that it takes a few minutes to catch up. It can leave you searching for your usual reaction; unable to comprehend why you are not feeling the same way. Obviously, this is an excellent indication, even if it does leave you slightly bewildered. It represents that the problem you are focusing on has become fragmented and the link with your emotional reactions has been broken.

## Calmness

Another common result of clearing the energy field is a feeling of calmness and well-being. A sense of inner peace may prevail and this indicates that a level of resolution has been reached and that a positive outcome will follow. Most people conclude their EFT session at this point.

## Experiencing the Healing Process

Now that you know what energetic sensations you may experience while applying the technique, what results can you expect in regard to your issue, phobia or physical complaint?

After the first round of EFT you should notice a reduction in emotional or physical intensity. For some, the problem falls away dramatically and can even vanish entirely. Simple issues that revolve around one subject will probably feel significantly different. For more complex ones, partial relief is achieved with the first round of EFT and subsequent round adjustments will be needed to complete the process.

It is common to discover another aspect to the problem, for instance, another emotion or different memory (*see* Chapter 6). This is a positive sign that healing is progressing in the right direction. As you repeat the technique you will observe emotional reactions becoming less intense until, finally, there should be no reaction at all – this is when your problem ceases to be a problem! An example of this can be illustrated with fears and phobias (*see* *Fig. 11*). Using a few rounds of EFT, you can expect a reduction of emotional intensity that follows a similar pattern to the one shown:

emotional healing

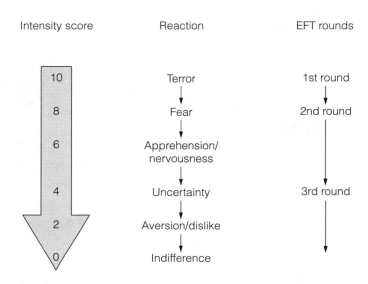

| Intensity score | Reaction | EFT rounds |
|---|---|---|
| 10 | Terror | 1st round |
| 8 | Fear | 2nd round |
| 6 | Apprehension/nervousness | |
| 4 | Uncertainty | 3rd round |
| 2 | Aversion/dislike | |
| 0 | Indifference | |

*Figure 11 – Dropping Intensity*

### julie's story – fear of wasps

Julie had always suffered from an intense fear of wasps. Every time the summer approached she would dread going outside. The buzzing sound of a wasp was all that was needed for her to run. Her fear was so intense that having a wasp in the same room or vicinity could provoke hysteria. Last spring we invited her to a demonstration evening. Julie decided to try it for her fear of wasps. She described her reaction as a 'ten out of ten' response. After the first round of EFT Julie's fear changed slightly and she now rated her fear at a level eight. The next round produced a marked difference and no matter how hard she tried she could not achieve a higher intensity level than a four out of ten. The third round completed the process. Overall it had taken her ten minutes. Later that summer, Julie realized that she hadn't been bothered by the presence of wasps. When one approached she felt different – instead of blind panic she now just didn't like wasps. She was no longer afraid and could quite happily let them buzz around her.

## Delayed Reactions

If immediate relief does not occur after a few rounds of EFT, changes sometimes appear a few hours or days later. Clients who have felt no initial improvement have experienced delayed benefits shortly after. Originally there may be very little response to the tapping process, but it is possible that the problem will gradually dissipate over the next few days. It is as though the body needs extra time to incorporate the adjustments that have been made before any of the benefits become apparent. Delayed results probably have more to do with a particular person's energy field or circumstances rather than the depth of the problem. So-called 'failed attempts' often prove extremely valuable a few days later.

## Changes in Perception

It has been our experience that clients frequently achieve insight into their limitations and often discover where they originate. It is difficult to be objective when your emotions are involved and they can cloud the issue and get in the way of seeing the whole picture. It is like looking at your situation through frosted glass. Once the emotional charge is reduced, you can see your circumstances clearly and with a more balanced outlook. People suddenly realize why they feel a certain way, or recognize the original cause of their problem.

emotional healing

# RESULTS AFTER'
# TREATMENT

Having cleared a phobia or emotion that you have experienced for a long time, you may wonder whether the results of the EFT treatment will hold out. In fact, they normally will because clearing the emotions serves to break the link between the trigger and the emotional response. Unless another unforeseen aspect to the problem surfaces, you should feel confident that the feelings have gone and will stay that way. Don't be surprised if you keep 'checking in' to see how you are feeling. If you have been responding in the same way for a long time, it can feel very strange to react differently. We become accustomed to avoiding certain situations and to being afraid, nervous and anxious. You will not always forget how terrified you were, or how resentful you felt before. It takes a while to break the habit. In the meantime, expect that you might initially search for your missing negative reaction until your confidence in the process grows.

## External Changes

All manner of external behaviours can reflect the internal changes that result from balancing the energy system. Changing your hairstyle, make-up and dress sense are all quite common. You may feel drawn to different colours or want to alter existing décor and furnishings. There can also be an urge to spring clean, indicating a strong desire to clear out the old and welcome the new. Equally, you could find yourself rearranging and sorting through old letters, photographs and keepsakes. You could notice that your eating habits, routines and social life alter. These events all illustrate at a very practical level the deep inner changes that are taking place.

## Other People's Reactions

We are often the last to notice the subtle shifts of energy that occur within ourselves. This is because the treatment does not involve adding anything, but instead returns us to a natural state of balance. When you have not seen someone else for a long time it is easy to notice how he or she has changed, even though they haven't. Energetic emotional clearing is a little like this. You may feel lighter, but are not able to put your finger on exactly what has altered.

Luckily, others often highlight for us the difference in our personality when they remark that we look different, younger or changed in some way. They may think that you have lost weight, had a haircut or been on holiday. This occurs because they can sense that you have changed, but cannot quite pinpoint what is different about you.

There can also be positive outcomes within relationships. The personal modifications that you make can have a subtle knock-on effect to those around you. As you work through the issues that challenge you in regard to others, you will find your relationships changing. Interactions can be closer, easier and more pleasant. The people we share our lives with will unconsciously register that we have altered. As you change, others around you quickly follow.

Dave wrote us an in-depth letter to explain the changes he had observed in his teenage daughter after just one EFT session:

### dave's story – teenage problems
'During the early part of this year, Isobel, my 15-year-old daughter, was experiencing many of the difficulties associated with teenagers. She had a number of minor setbacks at

school. She felt unappreciated in all that she attempted and she felt let down by a number of her friends whom she had trusted. It all amounted to a lack of self-esteem and the tendency to expect the worst-case scenarios of every forthcoming event.

'I have counselled young people for many years, but I made very little progress with my own daughter. In desperation I arranged an EFT session for Isobel. While driving to the appointment, I had to put up with a stream of negative comments from Isobel, such as "I am not talking to this woman" and "I'll give her two minutes and then I'm off". The treatment lasted about an hour and Isobel didn't have to disclose any of her problems, only tune into them.

'I didn't attend the session personally and am not sure what aspects were tapped for – I can only speak for the results. Everyone who knows my daughter remarked on her appearance. She was more relaxed, more positive, happy, outgoing and definitely a lot easier to get on with. Even her relationships with school friends returned to normal.

'In one afternoon Isobel was given a very special gift and she continues to use it whenever she feels it necessary. I also feel that as a family, we too were given a gift. We were given back our Isobel.'

# THE APEX EFFECT

Within Energy Psychology there is a characteristic known as 'The Apex Effect'. Essentially, this describes a reaction by which people forget the original intensity of their problem. Because issues can be resolved quickly, it becomes easy to rationalize the effects of the treatment or to overlook the improvements that have been made. Once an issue is resolved, we return to our normal balanced self and forget how we felt before the treatment. It can also be hard to conceive that such a simple technique can produce such profound changes. Many people attribute EFT's success to something quite unconnected such as:

'I was distracted.'
'It wasn't such a big deal anyway.'
'It was auto-suggestion.'
'I've done a lot of work on this problem already.'

The impact of energetic therapies is ignored as it does not fit the person's current model of the world. Because people have no reference point on which to hang EFT, they would rather explain the results away than admit that such a bizarre technique actually helped them. The Score Chart helps to avoid the Apex Effect, serving as a reminder of how intense each issue was and the improvements obtained with each EFT round.

# THE SCORE
## CHART

Before each round of EFT, the intensity of your issue is given a score from one to ten – each score is known as a 'Subjective Unit of Disturbance' (SUD). Ten represents the most extreme distress possible. If you describe your reaction as a ten out of ten you would probably feel immense fear and terror at the mere thought of approaching your ordeal. Equally, emotional pain, grief and betrayal can feel just as overwhelming. A score of one represents hardly any problem at all. Zero would indicate that you experience no emotional reaction whatsoever and that you feel calm and relaxed when you think about the original problem.

The Score Chart enables you to evaluate the extent of the problem, as well as monitor your progress. It gives you the chance to observe your problem diminishing and illustrates if more treatment is needed to eradicate the problem completely.

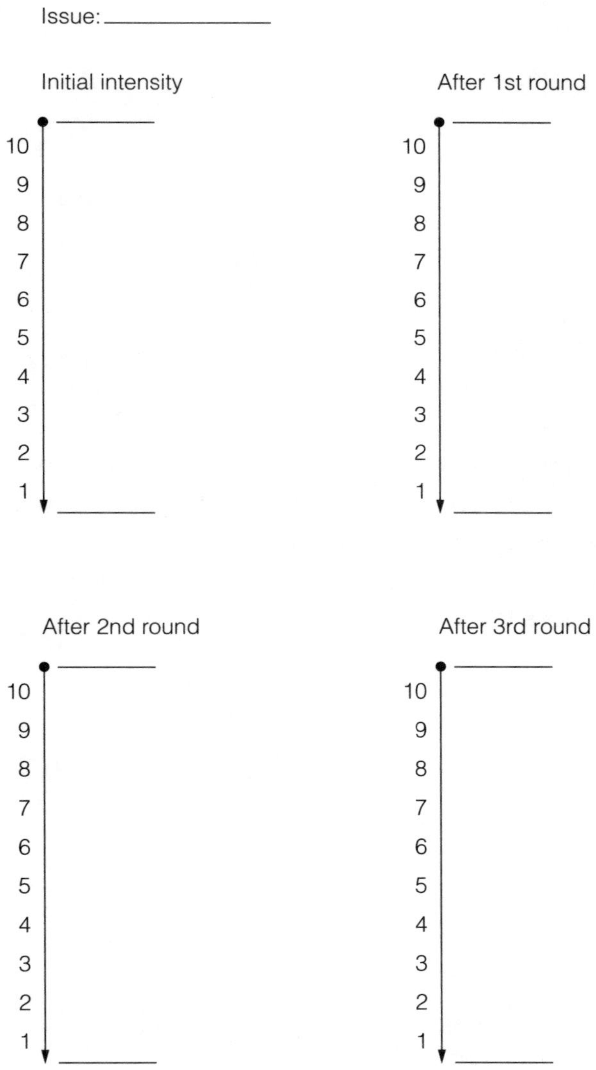

Issue: _____

Initial intensity

10
9
8
7
6
5
4
3
2
1

After 1st round

10
9
8
7
6
5
4
3
2
1

After 2nd round

10
9
8
7
6
5
4
3
2
1

After 3rd round

10
9
8
7
6
5
4
3
2
1

*Figure 12 – EFT Score Chart*

## Chapter 6

# Multiple Aspects

Some of the issues that you wish to resolve with EFT will involve multiple 'aspects'. To achieve the highest benefit from EFT, all aspects of a problem need to be cleared, one by one. For instance, if you work on a flying phobia you may discover various elements which, when combined together, generate a fear of flying. It is always essential to be as specific as possible when applying EFT and so tapping for the general statement '*My fear of flying*' will not produce the same results as tapping for all the particular aspects that make up your fear. So, first you need to identify these aspects; they might be something like this:

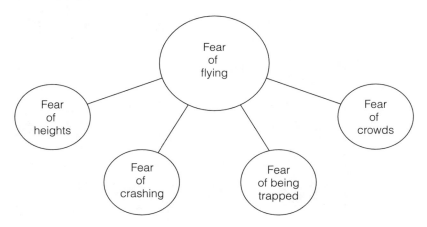

*Figure 13 – Fear of Flying*

After identifying each different element involved in a flying phobia, you then turn each aspect of the problem into a specific statement:

> 'Even though I am frightened of heights I deeply and completely accept myself.'
> 'Even though I feel claustrophobic in crowds I deeply and completely accept myself.'
> 'Even though I am frightened we will crash I deeply and completely accept myself.'
> 'Even though I feel trapped I deeply and completely accept myself.'

There are some problems that are very complex and contain multiple aspects and all of the specific elements that contribute to a problem will need to be addressed in order to release the entire feeling. An example of this is shown below.

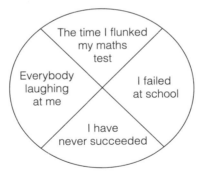

*Figure 14 – Aspects Involved in a Feeling of Failure*

To start with, if you had a fear of failure you could address it thus:

'Even though I feel a failure I deeply and completely accept myself.'

Then, to hone the treatment, specify the individual aspects that come to mind or provoke a reaction in relation to the feeling of failure:

'Even though I flunked my maths test I deeply and completely accept myself.'
'Even though everybody laughed at me I deeply and completely accept myself.'
'Even though I have never succeeded I deeply and completely accept myself.'
'Even though I failed at school I deeply and completely accept myself.'

Feelings connected to life-changing events such as relationship breakdown or grief can be equally as complex. This is because they evoke so many different feelings, memories, assumptions – as well as the practical problems to be dealt with.

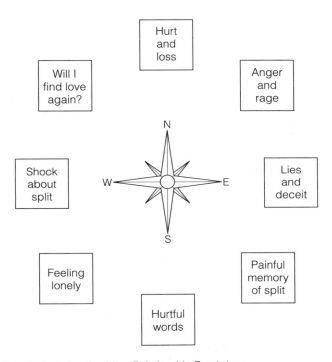

*Figure 15 – Aspects Involved in a Relationship Breakdown*

Experiences such as a relationship breakdown commonly produce several differing emotions at once, including anger, hurt, grief and disappointment. Each emotional response will need to be balanced in turn to remove the overall feeling. It is important to tap for the memories that come to light, as well as the thoughts you experience while connecting to the issue. Diffusing each one in turn will enable you to move forward much quicker with your healing process.

emotional healing

# HEALING
##   LAYERS

As you release each feeling, you may notice that another one surfaces. Originally you were feeling sad; after a few rounds of EFT you feel more angry than sad. This is a good response and indicates that you are working through the various layers of emotion. An analogy of this would be an iceberg. At first, we are only aware of the emotions that exist above the water; once this first layer is removed other feelings float up to the surface to be cleared in their turn.

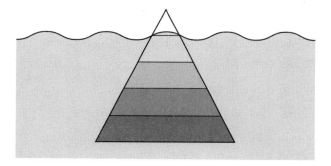

*Figure 16 – Iceberg Model of Submerged Emotions*

A similar process occurs if you use EFT for personal growth and life enhancement. Working through areas that have been holding you back enables deeper and more fundamental issues to come to the surface. By clearing the surface layers of fears, hurt and limitations, you allow deeper issues to emerge. This is like the layers of an onion being peeled away. Each time a layer is removed, a more fundamental and underlying issue comes to light. By continually clearing away emotional debris and out-dated beliefs, inner transformation and radical changes can occur. A new you is uncovered.

# LEVELS OF
## HEALING

The uppermost layers to our problems tend to be the most obvious. They contain the unpleasant symptoms from which we want relief. This level includes ailments such as blushing, weight-gain, emotional reactions, panic attacks and addictions. Most people are more than happy just to be free of this surface layer. Yet, without addressing the root cause of a problem, they could be leaving themselves vulnerable to its return. This could be seen as the *first* level of healing.

In some cases, healing would be incomplete if only these symptoms were removed. Once the symptoms have been resolved, underlying patterns and compensating behaviours are often highlighted. This might be the need for perfection, a desire to be in control, the way we use food or drugs to fill feelings of emptiness, or the constant need to please others. Working on these issues will underpin the progress already made. It will also serve to prevent a falling back into old patterns and recreating the original situation at some later date. Removing the underlying pattern of behaviour will produce a deeper and more consistent *second* level of healing.

Deeper still lie our unconscious beliefs, core issues and formative experiences. These tend to be the real causative factors of our behaviours. They are usually the furthest from our awareness, so we often remain oblivious to their existence. Childhood issues, painful memories and traumatic events are all stored here. At this level we also keep the more subtle beliefs and observations we make about the world. If we identify the deepest issue that needs to be healed, the more powerful the changes will be. Difficulties resolved at this *third* level will promote radical transformation and deep inner resolution.

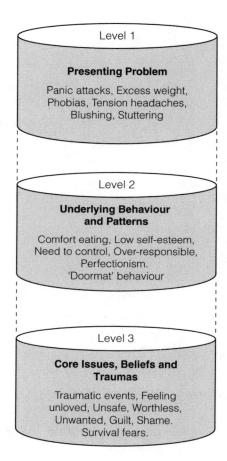

*Figure 17 – The Different Levels of Healing*

# DISCOVERING ALL YOUR ASPECTS

Finding all the aspects to a problem can take a little practice. Sometimes you will be able to pinpoint the various emotions and different facets to a problem quite easily. You may find that all the aspects surface while tapping without having to search for them – the first emotion making way for the next, a memory emerging, allowing a belief or a thought process to come to light. At other times it is more difficult, especially as our emotions can become confused and conflicting. For instance, you may have overcome the pain you felt at a friend's deceit, but forgiving that friend feels almost impossible. Initially, you may be unaware that this aspect to the situation is keeping you locked into the past. Until all aspects are removed, the memory will still contain an emotional charge and probably leave a bad taste in your mouth whenever you think about it. By releasing all of the aspects involved you will become completely free. You will not forget what happened, just feel more at peace with it because if it doesn't touch you anymore.

# DISCOVERING ASPECTS

After tuning into your problem, sit with a pen and paper and write down every thought, memory or feeling that enters your mind in relation to it. Even if what comes to mind seems irrelevant, write it down. Let your mind drift to all the different events and memories that may be related in some way. Be particularly aware of your self-talk. What do you say to yourself about the problem? Can you hear any comments from others? Do you experience any physical sensations when you think about it? Give each aspect a score out of ten to rate its intensity. Once you have written down as many aspects of the problem as you can think of, turn each one into a sentence and apply a round of EFT to the feeling until it diminishes.

## THE GENERALIZATION EFFECT

All the same, it is not always essential to identify every aspect contributing to your problem. Sometimes the energy system will automatically remove the entire issue after you have focused on just a few attributes. This is known as 'The Generalization Effect'. You could be tapping for a very specific item, only to find that the benefits have generalized to similar experiences as well. Even though your fear of spiders has various elements to it, tapping for just one or two of the main features can immediately collapse the whole phobia. Traumatic periods in your life, such as unhappiness during childhood, can include a hundred different memories and incidents that contribute to a feeling of sadness in adult life. Fortunately, the Generalization Effect can address clusters of memories and emotions collectively, reducing a hundred different tapping incidents to just ten or fifteen core issues. This is because there are main events and feelings around which all other thoughts and memories gather. Removing an issue at the foundation of the problem allows the others to fall away.

Sara's story illustrates how one emotion can have far reaching effects on all other areas of life. Sara's situation contained many aspects and layers of emotion. However one feeling prevailed over all the others – and that was guilt.

## sara's story – layers of guilt

'I had left my husband three and half years ago, after 23 years of marriage. My four children, aged between ten and seventeen, stayed with my ex-husband. Although the separation was amicable and I saw the children every two or three days, it caused me enormous pain and grief. However, it was a long time before I could acknowledge this because of the guilt I felt about leaving them. I had received a lot of homeopathic treatment and some counselling, and this helped me through the worst patches, but it was a slow process.

'Being used to homeopathy, where a lot of talking and investigation is involved, I was surprised how little pre-amble there was with EFT. After only a short discussion, I was asked what was troubling me most at that time. Without hesitation I said "The guilt over leaving my children", even though it had happened almost four years earlier. When I was asked what score I would give this feeling out of ten, I immediately answered "fifteen" and burst into tears! After two rounds of tapping I could not find the feeling of guilt anymore. Instead there was tremendous anger at my ex-husband. Then, in the following rounds this was dissolved and feelings of being rejected by him came up; then, much to my surprise, jealousy of him. Further tapping and quiet reflection revealed that I felt he had usurped my position in the family. He had become the son my parents always wanted. My mother would always support him before me and I was made to feel guilty for ever criticizing him. As the tapping proceeded I discovered further guilty feelings connected with my mother-in-law, who, I discovered, I actually hated! Gradually, over the following weeks, it became clear to me that I had been desperately trying to act as other people expected.

'Using EFT in further sessions, I worked on issues of self-confidence and esteem, anger and frustration with my partner, and the need to control and be over-responsible. Every time an emotion came up (and often before the end of each round) it would disappear or change to another feeling, which would then be tapped away. Finally, we would reach a point where I felt calm and comfortable and there would be a natural conclusion to the session.

'The effect of EFT goes on and on. Since being relieved of the guilt of leaving my children, I have developed better relationships with them than I have ever had. The immediate effect was that I felt I could "look them in the eye" again. We now have a straight forward, but deep love and respect for each other. As with them, all my other relationships improved immensely as a result.'

By removing the most powerful and disruptive emotional issue for Sara, the effect of the treatment had a generalizing and healing effect on every other part of her life. Addressing the core issue or central problem within a person's life can have a tremendously beneficial influence on all other areas.

## HIDDEN ASPECTS

When an issue appears to resist EFT, it is often because it contains aspects that have not yet been acknowledged or worked upon. It may seem that you still have exactly the same problem, but on closer inspection (and if you wrote down the original statements that you tapped for) you will probably discover that the previous aspect to the problem has gone. When you now focus on your issue, it is often a different element of the same situation that is causing distress. Repeating the EFT procedure for this new aspect will work just as well.

With future events there can also be aspects that are not anticipated. A good way to ensure that you have resolved most of the aspects that you are likely to encounter in a possible future event is to walk yourself through the situation in your mind. For instance, if you have an important exam coming up and just thinking about exams brings you out in a sweat, you could start by imagining each stage leading up to the exam that might cause you anxiety. Tap for the anxiety that occurs when you think about the exam, then any fears of failure or the fear of forgetting everything on the day. Visualize how you will feel a week before the exam date, if there are any uncomfortable feelings clear them straight away. Think about how you will feel the night before, in the morning, travelling to the exam centre, walking into the examination; turning over the paper and so on. Go through as many circumstances as you can think of prior to the actual exam. If any memories surface about previous examinations, clear the emotional charge connected to them. In this way you are addressing your fears and anticipations before the day. As a result you will probably find that you are much more relaxed about the prospect, feeling calm and more in control. If the feelings return or you come across another aspect that you hadn't thought of – for instance, the fear of being late – just reapply the technique. It only takes a few concentrated minutes of your time to gain relief.

Specifically focusing on one emotion or memory at a time allows an entire incident to be broken down into digestible pieces and eradicated systematically. By highlighting each individual aspect to a problem, you help the body to make sense of an often jumbled and confused ball of emotions.

## Chapter 7

# Psychological Reversal

While working with clients, Dr Callahan discovered an irregular energy state that he named 'Psychological Reversal'. It was the term he used to describe a form of polarity reversal within the meridians. When this situation exists, the energy system appears to work against the person's intentions. Any positive results of treatment plans, lifestyle changes or therapies (including EFT) are hampered, if not completely blocked by this condition. Ultimately, the reversal of energy flow creates the opposite of what you want.

Psychological Reversal is also one of the main reasons that both complementary and orthodox medicines sometimes fail. It also accounts for the repeated failure of attempts to improve a particular area of your life. Chronic disease, depression and addictions are all thought to contain an element of Psychological Reversal – the body being at odds with itself.

For example, you may wish to give up smoking and have tried every technique available. Yet, try as you might, you always end up admitting defeat and find yourself smoking again. This is a clear example of Psychological Reversal – you want one thing, but another part of you really wants something else.

Just as we can override our own conscience when we do things that we know are harmful to us – such as eating the wrong foods or drinking too much – our energy system can also override our good intentions when we are trying to overcome an emotional problem, or commit to a new lifestyle.

Psychological Reversal is a form of self-sabotage that occurs at an uncon-scious level. You may have one intention in mind – for instance, to lose weight – but your unconscious mind and therefore your energy system has another idea in mind – to gain weight.

We all have varying degrees of Psychological Reversal in our lives. It is not a personal fault or character flaw and it happens quite unconsciously. It takes place in response to negative thoughts, depression, ingrained beliefs, self-defeating limitations and concealed psychological agendas. These deep-rooted responses affect the energy system in a dramatic way. They are often the result of distressing childhood experiences, traumatic inci-dents, conditioning and the observations and decisions we make about life. Although subtle, these factors can have a very powerful influence on the way our energy system functions and on the outcome we desire. When present, this kind of negative programming can block positive intentions and keep us locked into problems we are trying our best to resolve. Consequently, the correct energy flow through the body is paramount to accomplishing your goal.

There are many different types of Psychological Reversal. Some people's energy systems are in constant reversal, leaving them in chronic disease states or emotional distress. Others may only experience energetic reversal when it comes to a particular issue. Either way, reversed energy flow will block progress and positive changes, until it's cleared.

Here are some of the common examples of self-sabotage that cause Psychological Reversal. If any of these statements cause you to feel uncom-fortable or cringe, it could indicate that they are good emotionally charged statements to work on.

# HIDDEN PSYCHOLOGICAL AGENDAS

## Beliefs

'I'm not psychologically reversed, I really want to get over this!'
'I don't believe I can get better/recover/get over this.'
'I don't believe that the condition I've got can be healed/changed.'
'I don't believe that EFT can help me.'
'It's too hard … too difficult … I can't …'
'Nothing has worked before.'

## Permissions

'I can't allow myself to heal totally (because "I feel guilty, unworthy or undeserving").'
'I don't love myself enough to let this go.'
'I'm not ready to get over this problem.'

## Safety

'I won't have an excuse without the problem.'
'I would fear the world or life without my problem.'
'I won't have to discover that I'm a failure if I don't try.'
'This fear keeps me safe/protects me.'

## Other People

'Will I still get the same level of support/attention from others?'
'Others won't allow me to change, they prefer me as I am.'
'It will cause too much upheaval.'
'I'm alright, it's them that need to change.'

## Effort

'Better the devil you know.'
'Too much effort to pull it off.'
'Too lazy.'
'Can't be bothered.'

## Self-concept

'I've always been like this.'
'I won't know who I am without this.'
'I might have to change.'
'I can't change, this is just the way I am.'
'I must have done something wrong, it must be my fault.'
'Things never work for me.'
'If I keep these feelings I get to punish them/be right/feel superior.'
'I'm justified in my feeling resentful, therefore I'm keeping it!'
'I always fail.'

## Other Pay-offs

'I get to be self-righteous.'

'I get more attention if I'm ill.'

'I like others feeling sorry for me.'

'If I get over this I'll have to go to school/ go out to work.'

'Who will help me if I get over this?'

'I enjoy it too much.'

As you can see, these hidden psychological factors can put a very real obstacle in the way of your success. They prevent healing from occurring and keep emotional and physical problems in place. The unconscious mind is working contrary to your conscious desire, ruining any opportunity for change. An appropriate analogy for this would be a set of scales – on the one side there are all the positive reasons why it is beneficial to be free of your problem, on the other side are all the unconscious blocks and resistance to losing it.

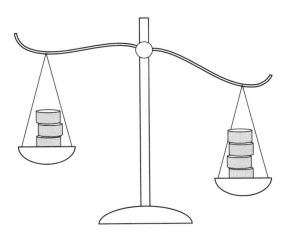

Stop smoking

1 Good for health
2 Save money
3 Fresher breath

Keep smoking

1 I enjoy it
2 It relaxes me
3 I've always smoked
4 I would feel awkward
   without cigarettes

*Figure 18 – Hidden Agendas – The Desire to Stop Smoking*

In the example above, there are more hidden pay-offs for remaining a smoker than there are for becoming a non-smoker. The chips are stacked against successfully overcoming a smoking addiction. You are more likely to set yourself up to fail than accomplish your goal. Paradoxically, through avoiding stopping you gain more than you lose.

Psychological Reversal often prevents clients from turning up for their pre-booked sessions. There is a part of them that genuinely fears the treatment succeeding. In our clinic there are more cancellations from people who want to give up smoking than anything else. You wouldn't believe some of the excuses people give! The unconscious fear of living without cigarettes far outweighs the conscious desire to stop.

Almost any issue can hold this type of unconscious trade-off. Essentially, the system perceives that it would cause the person to lose out in some way and refuses to give permission for a problem to be resolved. If the resolution of a habit or problem involves facing feelings of anxiety or if it requires mountains of effort, it may not serve the person to change. The benefits that exist in this form of trade-off are that you don't have to change, leave your comfort zone or challenge yourself. Inevitably, the price you pay is to keep your problem, as well as possibly damaging your health!

This can apply to any area of life, relationships, career and, particularly, money matters. If you are psychologically reversed on the issue of making money, it will be very hard to become rich. Most of us would like to have more money, but often we have unconscious beliefs that work against us, such as:

'There is never enough.'
'I'm no good with money.'
'None of my family ever had money.'
'Too much money is bad.'
'I wouldn't know what to do if I was rich.'
'Rich people are selfish.'
'Life's a struggle.'
'There are always bills to pay.'
'It couldn't happen to me.'
'Only educated people have money.'

Unconscious programmes such as these will make it almost impossible to be financially successful. Our energy configuration becomes wired up to create the opposite of what we would like to happen, making sure that every time money comes into our lives, it leaves just as quickly. This is because being financially successful would go against everything we believe. It may feel uncomfortable to be rich, as if it doesn't fit our model of the world or ourselves. We may want more money but our negative self-concept will prevent it from happening. Neutralizing these beliefs can help you attract, rather than repel, money into your life. Each belief is equivalent to an emotionally-charged statement that can be easily transformed through the tapping process.

## Outdated Beliefs

There are some problems that are extremely uncomfortable to live with and it is not clear how they can benefit you in any way. In these cases, the aspects of you that are in conflict are often quite outdated. They can be born of decisions made in crisis or of beliefs formed as a small child. If as a child you were punished for questioning authority, a core belief could have been installed dictating, *'If I question authority, I will be punished'*. In this case, any situation that involves challenging authority will feel scary, if not out – right dangerous! The perceived consequences of standing up for yourself will appear much worse than anything you might expect to gain. As a result, it may feel better to stay as you are rather than rock the boat. Consequently, the childhood belief continues to dictate your adult behaviour and ruins any chance of acting differently.

Equally, if you made a decision to *'Never trust men'*, after your first love cheated on you, finding a secure relationship with a man in the future could pose difficulties. Your energy will continue to attract men who are untrustworthy until you stop trying to prove yourself right! There is a strong possibility that Psychological Reversal would prevent you from letting go of this belief, as the unconscious mind perceives that this principle keeps you safe. As the memory of being hurt was so unbearable, an unconscious trade-off is to remain single. In this way, you benefit from avoiding disappointment and

emotional healing

heartache, yet you also lose a great deal. Although it may be difficult to admit, many people remain on their own because they secretly fear being emotionally hurt. Before being able to trust again, the psychological barrier that prevents this needs to be replaced by something more appropriate. Being in a healthy and happy relationship is far more important than being a martyr to ingrained beliefs! Adjusting the energy system can help to clear the fear of trusting, enabling you to enjoy much more than just the avoidance of pain.

# DEALING WITH PSYCHOLOGICAL REVERSAL

Luckily, Psychological Reversal can be corrected. In most cases, the first part of the tapping procedure, 'The Set-up', will remove it. The Set-up was designed to ensure that what you desire and your unconscious beliefs are in agreement. Repeating the *'Even though ... I deeply and completely accept myself'* affirmation neutralizes negativity connected to the issue. It also promotes a positive openness and receptivity to change. Even if Psychological Reversal is not apparent, the correction technique is built in to the EFT process and it will usually counterbalance the reversal of energy flow.

## Fear of Fear

There are some complex or deeply ingrained beliefs that may need a little extra attention before working on the issue at hand. A prime example is not wanting to overcome a fear of heights, because it might mean having to face going up a ladder in the process (and that's the very thing you fear most!). In this instance, the resistance to getting over the problem will need to be cleared, prior to attempting to work on the actual fear of heights. This form of Psychological Reversal is a *fear* of facing the fear.

It is a back-to-front logic that makes perfect sense to your unconscious mind. If the fear is kept intact, you save yourself from any additional fear that may result from confronting the problem. With EFT, clearing a phobia is never about facing your fear with gritted teeth and clenched fists. That is what happens normally and it can be terrifying – as well as exhausting! EFT serves to break the link between the fear response and the perceived threat, prior to attempting to address the actual situation. The person with the height phobia would not be facing their worst fear at all. They would experience minimal or no response at all when faced with a ladder. But first the unconscious mind needs to be convinced and the energy flow altered that prevents them from even attempting to leave first base.

# DISCOVERING POSSIBLE PSYCHOLOGICAL REVERSAL

Although most Psychological Reversal exists beyond our conscious awareness, it is possible to discover some of our hidden agendas. If we truly question our own motives and intentions, we can often find negative obstacles that we have unknowingly put in our way. Write down as many reasons as you can think of why you are unable to get over your issue, physical discomfort or trauma. Be as honest as you can with yourself. Make sure you use as many excuses as you usually do.

## Weighing Up the Pros and Cons

A clear example of Psychological Reversal can be illustrated by drawing your own set of scales. Think of the issue you would like freedom from. On one side of the scales place all the positive reasons that you have for achieving your goal. On the other side, list every reason, requirement or negative thought that prevents you.

Problems that have more positive gains than negative are often quite easily resolved. Issues that have more reasons 'not to' are likely to be extremely tough to solve without addressing the hidden incentives first. Next, we come to a method that will test whether you are psychologically reversed on a particular issue. You may like to compare your own list with the discoveries you make through this method.

## Muscle Testing

Muscle testing is a rather fun way of discovering whether Psychological Reversal is holding you back. Our energy system responds rapidly to our thoughts and these subtle energy shifts are automatically picked up throughout the body. Because it is impossible for our body and our energy fields to lie, it is possible to obtain a good insight into your unconscious intentions by asking your body. If you are asked a series of questions about your problem, your answers will register throughout your energy system. Your physical responses to these questions will then disclose information and hidden 'truths'. Muscle testing can illustrate the influence that positive and negative thoughts have on our body. In this way, you can use this simple practice to uncover essential blocks to achieving your goals.

# EXERCISE 1 –
## MUSCLE TESTING

You will need to team up with a trusted friend for this exercise. First of all, make sure you are both comfortable with using muscle testing. In order to do this, and to gauge a basic positive and negative response from the body, stand facing each other. Clear your minds and be totally receptive to what you may discover. To make sure that you don't influence each other it is best to avoid eye contact. Remain neutral and non-judgmental to the results.

**1**  If you are the person to be tested, stand with your feet apart. Hold your left arm straight out to the side at right angles to the body, with your thumb pointing towards the floor. This is the testing position.

**2**  Your partner is now going to ask you to repeat some simple statements to which you know that the answer is 'yes', such as:

'My name is —-'
'I am wearing a blue shirt.'
'I am 39 years old.'
'My daughter's name is —-'
'I am a financial advisor.'

Once you have repeated the completed statement, your partner will use two fingers to apply gentle pressure to the wrist of your upheld arm. This is not a test of strength – the force needs to be firm, but not enough to overpower the individual. To let you know they are about to apply pressure they will say '*Resist*' or '*Hold*'. Your job is simply to resist their pressure.

If you have managed to resist successfully you will have obtained a positive *'Yes, this is true'* indication from the body. The most likely reaction is for your muscle to lock and resist the pressure to move the arm down. The arm may move ever so slightly at the introduction of pressure, but it will probably hold tight after the first few seconds. This response can then be used as the benchmark for all statements that your body and unconscious mind believe to be true.

**3** Now repeat the whole process for statements that you know require a definite 'no' answer:

'My name is Father Christmas.'
'I am eight years old.'
'I am a billionaire.'
'I live in the Antarctic.'

The results of this test should be very clearly different from the first. When testing the body, a *'No, this is not true'* response should elicit an arm that can be pushed down with very little effort. A 'yes' is usually represented by a strong resistant arm, a 'no' by a weak, limp arm. Have a few practice sessions until you feel quite happy with evaluating the results. Once you have established which response represents a 'yes' or 'no' answer, you are ready to discover if Psychological Reversal is a problem for the issue you are working with.

# EXERCISE 2 –
## MUSCLE TESTING
# FOR PSYCHOLOGICAL
## REVERSAL

**1** Once again, stand with your feet apart. The left arm is then held straight out to the side at right angles with the body, the thumb pointing towards the floor.

**2** Your partner will now test you for a series of statements about the issue you wish to clear. A good place to start is by stating what you want to achieve, as well as the opposite of what you desire, to see which one has the strongest response. Say aloud a statement that relates to your situation. For instance:

'I want to lose weight/I want to gain weight.'
'I want to change/I want to stay as I am.'
'I believe I can get better/I don't believe I can get better.'
'I deserve to get over this …/I don't deserve to get over this.'
'I want to resolve this fear/I want to keep this fear.'

Also test for any area that may be preventing you from fully resolving your issue:

'I forgive myself for what happened/I forgive others for what happened.'

'I like being a "poor me".'
'It is safe for me to let go of this.'
'It is in my best interest to resolve this.'

Each time a statement is made, your partner will apply gentle pressure to your extended wrist and tell you to 'resist'. If the statement is true, your arm will remain strong and unmovable. If the statement is false your arm will be weak and easily pushed down. If the body indicates that an unconscious part of you is resisting something that you consciously desire, then Psychological Reversal is present. Write down what you discover.

## WHAT IS YOUR TRUTH? – VOC TEST

An alternative to Muscle testing is the 'Truth Test', commonly known as a Validity of Cognition (VOC) Test.

## EXERCISE – VOC SCALE

If you suspect that Psychological Reversal is preventing your progress, spend some time identifying any beliefs, thoughts or attitudes that are in conflict with resolving your issue. Once you have a list of statements, give each one a score from one to ten, relating to how true each one seems to you. This may be a little difficult at first but just estimate or guess how strongly you believe each statement. Absolutely true would be ten, fairly accurate would be five and a complete lie would be zero. Go through the examples on the previous pages as well as rating any thoughts of your own that have come to light. When you have done this, write it down as in the example below.

| Negative Statement | How True it Feels |
| --- | --- |
| 'I will never amount to anything.' | 8/10 |
| 'I will never find a decent job.' | 6/10 |
| 'I can't overcome this.' | 7/10 |
| 'It couldn't possibly work for me.' | 9/10 |
| 'I enjoy having others look after me.' | 5/10 |
| 'Having this problem gives me an excuse.' | 9/10 |
| 'I want others to do it for me.' | 8/10 |

Rating the level of belief in each conflicting thought gives you a rough idea of how intense the energy block is within each one. The higher the score, the more negative the interference will be. It also gives you a guideline to refer back to after correcting each belief with EFT. Ideally, as a problem resolves the negative statement should receive a very low score, if not a zero.

The VOC test works in the opposite direction to a SUD scale. It is designed to monitor your level of belief in a statement, rather than the emotional intensity. After a few minutes of energy balancing, the negative truth should become an untruth after just a little tapping!

A VOC test can also be used to measure your confidence once a distressing issue has diminished. If a problem fails to create an emotional disturbance of any kind on the SUD scale, it can be helpful to measure your response with a VOC test. The VOC scale can assess the level of truth in both positive and negative statements. Here are some positive statements to practise on. Rate each one individually, giving yourself zero if it is completely untrue, five points if it is fairly accurate, and ten points if it is absolutely true.

> 'I feel happy.'
> 'I deserve to get over this problem.'
> 'I am successful.'
> 'I am confident.'
> 'I feel completely at ease with spiders/flying/heights.'
> 'I am important.'
> 'I feel comfortable with my physical appearance.'
> 'I feel relaxed.'
> 'I deserve to be wealthy.'
> 'I feel safe.'

Once a problem has been addressed successfully, a positive statement should attain a high score of belief. If the level of belief in the positive attribute you desire is relatively low, it indicates that there is still some work to do in this area.

## Psychological Reversal Correction

It is important that the statements you work with create an emotional charge. They need to be sentences that best describe the unconscious gains and reasons for staying in your current situation. The more exact they are, the easier it is to eliminate any psychological agenda that holds an issue in place. To balance the conflicting energy flow caused by Psychological Reversal and to remove the influence it has on your progress, you will need to do some EFT adjustments to eradicate the unconscious gains. For instance, if you muscle test positive for:

> 'I want to stay as I am.'

a good statement to use could be

> 'Even though I want to stay as I am I deeply and completely accept myself.'

If your unconscious mind feels that holding on to a particular fear keeps you safe and you believe this to be a nine out of ten truth, you could state:

> 'Even though my fear keeps me safe I deeply and completely accept myself.'

Focusing on the unconscious gain will allow the tapping to dissolve its influence. If after a few rounds of EFT the problem remains intact, it can indicate the presence of a deep form of Psychological Reversal, which requires specific targeting to correct. To enhance your results, create a statement that includes the fact that a part of you wants to stay as you are, such as:

> 'Even though I want to remain angry I deeply and completely accept myself.'
> 'Even though I am unwilling to forgive them I deeply and completely accept myself.'
> 'Even though I don't really want to get over my spending habit I deeply and completely accept myself.'
> 'Even though I don't want to change I deeply and completely accept myself.'

Apply an entire round of EFT to the thoughts that are preventing you suc-ceeding. After a few adjustment rounds for the Psychologically Reversed statement, ask your partner to test you again. This time you could measure your level of belief in both the positive and negative versions of the relevant statement to see which one is more accurate. You should notice that by addressing your internal conflict specifically, energy reversal is corrected. When you now state your desire, such as

'I want to be free of my craving for chocolate.'

the muscle test indicates that your body agrees with you. Testing for:

'I don't want to be free of my craving for chocolate.'

causes the body to disagree, indicating that all parts of you are ready to release your craving.

Once Psychological Reversal has been cleared, the energy system is open to influence. Problems will now respond in the usual way to the basic tapping procedure. Complete as many rounds as you need to in order to negate the beliefs that are interfering with your desired outcome. Tune into the negative block that prevents you from overcoming your problem. As you tap, observe any signs of energy shifts taking place. Continue until you feel the statement is no longer true, or the level of emotional intensity drops to a zero.

Hopefully, you will not need to undo the hidden agendas that lay behind the issues. Most problems will respond to the basic EFT procedure without the need for double thinking your predicament. However, if you find that after several attempts to reduce your discomfort the intensity level remains pretty much the same, it can be assumed that there is an underlying benefit that exists on another level. Finding out exactly what negative thoughts are holding you back will give you a much greater chance to rid yourself finally of what has been troubling you. It will also prevent the internal tug-of-war that creates conflicting messages about what you want to achieve. When all your parts are pulling in the same direction, you will experience much faster and longer-lasting results.

## Chapter 8

# The Self-help Approach

It is now time to put everything you have learnt into practice. To build your confidence in EFT, the first issue you choose to work on needs to be something quite specific. An easily definable emotion or situation is the best place to start.

## Step 1 – Identify the Problem

Select an issue where you can immediately gauge or notice an improvement, such as a current irritation, a situation that annoys you or a phobic response.

## Step 2 – Formulate a Statement

Formulate a specific statement that best describes how you feel.

## Step 3 – Score Chart

Grade the feeling or sensation from one to ten pertaining to how intense it is, ten being extremely severe, one being fairly minimal.

## Step 4 – Affirmation Link Up

Rub the tender spot on your upper chest or tap the Karate Chop point while repeating the affirmation three times.

'Even though I … [problem] … I deeply and completely accept myself.'

## Step 5 – Reminder Phrase

Now shorten the affirmation to a simple reminder phrase or word:

'This hurt'
'This guilt'
'This stiff pain'
'This headache'

## Step 6 – Tapping points

Tap each point seven times while repeating the reminder phrase and thinking about the specific feature you wish to clear.

| | |
|---|---|
| Eyebrow | EB |
| Side of Eye | SE |
| Under the Eye | UE |
| Under the Nose | UN |
| Chin | Ch |
| Collarbone | Cb |
| Under the Arm | UA |

| Thumb | Th |
| Index Finger | IF |
| Middle Finger | MF |
| Little Finger | LF |
| Karate Chop | KC |

Take a deep breath in and then out.

## Step 7 – The Gamut

Simultaneously tap the Gamut point while performing the following steps:

1 Close your eyes.
2 Open your eyes.
3 While keeping your head perfectly still look hard down right.
4 While keeping your head perfectly still look hard down left.
5 Look right again.
6 Look left again.
7 Roll your eyes in an anti-clockwise direction.
8 Repeat in a clockwise direction.
9 Take a deep breath.

## Step 8 – The Second Sequence

Repeat the tapping sequence using the reminder phrase as before:

| | |
|---|---|
| Eyebrow | EB |
| Side of Eye | SE |
| Under the Eye | UE |
| Under the Nose | UN |
| Chin | Ch |
| Collarbone | Cb |
| Under the Arm | UA |
| Thumb | Th |
| Index Finger | IF |
| Middle Finger | MF |
| Little Finger | LF |
| Karate Chop | KC |

## Step 9 – Reassessment

Tune into your issue again and score the current intensity level. If the issue has completely faded you can stop there. If there is still some work to be done, proceed to Step 10. If another aspect to your problem is prominent return to Step 1 and apply the technique to this aspect.

## Step 10 – Round Adjustments

Now repeat the entire procedure as many times as necessary to release the remaining feelings, using the affirmation:

> 'Even though I still have some remaining feelings of
> … I deeply and completely accept myself.'

with a reminder phrase that includes the word *remaining*.

'Remaining hurt'
'Remaining headache'

# MONITORING YOUR PROGRESS

Keeping a check on your results should be pretty straightforward if you make a list of statements and score levels as you go. After every session, go back through the list of statements to assess how you feel about each one. The emotional intensity of each statement should reduce until the score reaches zero. Aim for very low scores, preferably zero, to ensure total resolution. At this stage there should be a significant reduction, if not a complete absence, of the original problem. If you have been successful the emotional discomfort will rapidly subside. None of the statements should now cause you any emotional reaction.

## New Aspects

Pay attention to any energy shifts that occur during the process – these are good indications of disrupted energy being cleared from the system. The best results are the ones that hold up in everyday life. Be assured that once you feel totally resolved about an issue, the emotional intensity will not return. The only situation that may provoke a reaction is a previously unrecognized aspect to the issue coming to the surface. By keeping a list of all your statements, you should be able to see that the current response is a new aspect requiring a different statement. If this happens, re-apply the technique as before.

As long as the first aspect you tapped for has cleared, making way for a different slant to the same problem, you are making progress. Each time you resolve a particular characteristic of fear or an emotional concern, you are reducing the overall problem. Moving through the various layers of a problem will remove it piece by piece and after a few rounds of tapping will lead to resolution.

Nevertheless, some problems may need persistence. This is especially the case for deeply ingrained habits and these may require daily tapping sessions to ensure the energy system sustains the changes. Addictions, weight loss and cravings will also need more than one application.

If you are one of a small number of people who does not experience an immediate reduction in emotional intensity, turn to the Troubleshooting section (*see* Chapter 16). You may also need to address Psychological Reversal (*see* Chapter 7) prior to treating the main issue.

## Dealing with Persistent Problems

Initially, issues that have a maintaining cause may also require a similar approach. For example, a work situation that is causing a lot of stress is likely to be unresponsive to just one tapping session because the very next day you will be subject to more stress. Yet if you use the tapping technique consistently you should notice that your response to your difficulties changes, even when the situation itself has not. In this way, EFT can become part of your strategy for stress management and, in time, the major benefits of the technique will become apparent.

General conditions such as low self-esteem or feelings of depression will also require several tapping sessions, as these feelings are usually a consolidation of multiple aspects and circumstances. They are usually the result of a number of events, memories, and ongoing situations contributing to an overall feeling and this will need to be broken down into aspects and addressed individually. As you gain skill and proficiency with EFT, these problems can be resolved. When issues appear to be extremely complex, this only indicates that there are more aspects to the problem than usual and by addressing each aspect in turn you will ultimately produce the required result. Every time a different aspect is neutralized, the overall negative condition will weaken, each tapping session peeling away another healing layer.

## Physical Problems

Physical complaints can also take time to heal. Balancing the energy system will create the right conditions for healing to take place. It will also be of tremendous help in alleviating pain and physical discomfort on a daily basis. We have received reports of people achieving freedom from the symptoms of many chronic conditions which have previously defied intervention. It may take three months of persistent tapping but there is little to lose. Apply EFT to all your physical problems, even the ones that you think it couldn't possibly help. You may be astonished by the healing capacity of the body when it is given the right circumstances.

# FUTURE EVENTS

After gaining relief from current problems or past events, you may like to apply EFT to a future event that you feel apprehensive about or that you know will be difficult for you. Future reactions are always hard to gauge. It is always a good idea to eliminate as many current uncomfortable feelings as possible prior to the event. It is also best to tap for your feelings the moment they arise. As soon as you start to feel anxious, tap straight away – don't wait until you're really suffering. The longer you leave it, the more emotional energy becomes involved.

## Dealing with Future Difficulties

Once you feel indifferent to the anticipated situation, it is likely you will sail through the actual event without any problems. Often, by removing your reaction to a perceived situation in the future, you also break the link with the actual situation. For example, you may be concerned about shaking or sweating profusely during an interview. After addressing each issue specifically, the fear either ceases to be a problem – so you stop worrying about the possibility of it happening – or the emotional reaction connected to the negative thought dissipates. The thought may still be there, but it won't cause any emotional response, thus allowing you to feel balanced and relaxed.

If you are using EFT for future events, the best way to test how you will respond is to vividly imagine yourself going through the situation step by step. It could be the moment you enter the room, or once all the attention turns to you. It could be a thought such as *'Oh no, what if ...'* or a memory that is triggered. Whatever aspect disturbs your equilibrium, tap for it immediately. At each stage check how you feel. If at any time you experience a surge of anxiety or feel uncomfortable, apply an additional round of EFT for that specific aspect. Continue to do this until you can visualize yourself going through the entire experience without any negative emotional responses whatsoever. Once you can picture yourself calmly coping with each stage of the event, you have successfully dissipated the emotional connection to the situation.

### louise's story – wedding nerves

'Last year I was a bridesmaid for a friend. The day before her wedding I was a gibbering wreck. I tried all sorts of pills but I didn't calm down until the wedding actually began. I didn't want this to happen again, especially not on my own wedding day.

'Up until a week before I was due to get married I was fine, but as it got closer I was a bag of nerves! I knew I was nervous, but could not pinpoint exactly why. So the first thing I tapped for was *"Even though I don't know why I am nervous I deeply and completely accept myself."* This opened a couple of doors.

'I suddenly felt very excited which caused my stomach to be in a state of turmoil. So the next statement I used was *"Even though my stomach is full of butterflies I deeply and completely accept myself."* This very quickly calmed me down.

'Once I had relaxed another emotion surfaced. Earlier in the year I had lost my Nan. The sole purpose for bringing forward the wedding day was for her. As I realized this, I had a sudden rush of sadness about the fact that she was not going to be there. I quickly worded my next statement, *"Even though my Nan cannot physically be with me on my wedding day I deeply and completely accept myself and know that she will be there in spirit, in my thoughts and in my heart."* After the first round my sadness lifted, not all together, but significantly.

'I then re-focused on my wedding day and had a sudden rush of anxiety. Once again I tapped for *"These anxious feelings."* Within a few minutes my nerves had vanished.

'EFT helped me a great deal to overcome my pre-wedding jitters – and a lot quicker than I expected. The night before, I slept like a baby. On the day itself I was as cool as a cucumber. It was great to feel so excited without being at all scared.'

Louise approached her anxiety by focusing on her physical sensations and the painful emotional connections that were triggered every time she thought about her wedding day. This is a great case in point because with weddings there are so many fine details and arrangements that have the potential to cause anxiety, as well as many profound emotional dimensions.

# EMERGENCY TREATMENT

If you find yourself in an unforeseen situation that is emotionally overwhelming, such as shock, fright or panic, you can apply the tapping sequence without a statement or the Set-Up. This is because you are experiencing energetic disruption to such a degree that it is not necessary to name the problem or address reversed energy flow. In emergency situations it is not essential to repeat a reminder phrase or even say anything at all. Just start tapping immediately. Going straight through the tapping sequence will be sufficient to balance the extreme reaction. Alanah wrote to us describing how she used EFT while experiencing an intense panic attack.

### alanah's story – traumatic memory: panic attack

'I was watching a very violent film about a kidnap late one night. It triggered a memory of a relationship that I had many years ago, in which my boyfriend had held me hostage with a knife. I remembered how I endured the whole experience by hiding under the duvet cover, shivering in terror. I was convinced that I would be dead by the morning.

'By the time the film had finished, my mind was completely consumed by the memory. I couldn't stop running through the events in my mind. I found myself under the duvet shivering in terror, just as I had that night. My heart was pounding so hard that I thought it was going to burst. I couldn't stop the tears. All the time my thoughts were getting louder and louder, I was terrified. I live alone and didn't feel able to phone anyone because it was about three in the morning. Besides, I'm not sure I would have made much sense.

'Finally, after several hours of panic and terror I remembered about EFT. I was tired and exhausted and could only manage to do one round of tapping and then it was only a few points on the face and collarbone. I couldn't even muster a statement or words to describe how I was feeling. It felt like quite a feeble attempt but the results were remarkable. Almost instantly I felt the part of me that was clinging on to the traumatic memory let go. My thoughts became quieter and quieter, I lay there observing my heartbeat slowing down, returning to its natural rhythm. I must have fallen asleep, because the next thing I knew it was morning. I was relieved and felt completely back to my normal self. 'On reflection other issues were also resolved. All my self-blame had gone;

it was now replaced with positive feelings about myself and my future relationships.'

Alanah's experience shows how effective EFT can be in emergency situations. At times like this, thinking clearly can be extremely difficult. Your emotions seem to be out of control and riding roughshod over any rational thoughts or actions. Simply tapping the meridian points can be all that is needed when emotions overpower you. Because you are so focused on the problem, there is no need to say anything or to remind yourself what you are tapping for. Just go straight ahead with the tapping until the crisis passes.

# part 3

# Emotional Healing in Practice

# Chapter 9

# Phobias

Irrational and bizarre as they may seem, phobias are no laughing matter to the sufferer. They can impair the ability to function and limit everyday life as the person attempts to avoid the object of their fear. Phobias are unsettling at the best of times, completely devastating at worst. When fear takes over, some people can be left with a very miserable and narrow existence. Many suffer in silence, as they are too embarrassed to admit to their feelings.

A phobia can reduce even the most courageous of us to a quivering wreck, leaving us unable to cope or regain self-control. Phobias come in all shapes and sizes; some of the more familiar include:

| | |
|---|---|
| bats | dark |
| bees | dentists |
| being alone | dirt |
| birds | dogs |
| blood | driving |
| cats | drowning |
| choking | dying |
| computers | enclosed spaces |
| creepy crawlies | exams |
| crossing bridges | flying |
| crowds | germs |

| | |
|---|---|
| getting fat | snakes |
| ghosts | socializing |
| heights | spiders |
| hospitals | supermarkets |
| illness | thunderstorms |
| injections | trains |
| leaving the house | using public toilets |
| lifts | vomiting |
| pins | water |
| public speaking | worms |

A phobia is defined as a persistent and irrational fear of a specific object or situation, coupled with the strong desire to avoid that object or situation. In fact, fear of facing the fear or of losing control can develop into yet another phobia in itself.

Most people recognize when their fears are irrational and out of proportion, yet the feelings of terror remain very real. When confronted with the object of their fear, their body quickly reacts with the classic fight-or-flight response – pounding heart, hyperventilation, sweating, dizziness and sometimes a full-blown panic attack.

Because phobias seem to manifest at a deeper level of consciousness, these excessive fear reactions seem to defy logic and reason. It is also common that traumatic experiences in the past can cause phobic respons- es in later life. Yet many people have no idea when or where their phobia began.

Phobias, fears and anxieties can be treated quickly and with minimal dis- tress. Just as with all other negative emotions, a phobic response creates a disruption in the body's energy system. Once rebalanced, the emotional charge and distress is rapidly released, leaving the person free from the troubling thoughts or uncomfortable emotions that contribute to a phobic condition. Once the fearful reaction to the object is removed, the person is able to form positive new thoughts and associations with the situation.

Some fears are not completely unfounded – heights, snakes, wasps and some forms of spider can be dangerous and it would be advisable to err on the side of caution – but EFT only diffuses emotional reactions that are unnecessary or overwhelming, it is impossible for it to remove natural caution.

To remove a phobia, you do not have to face your fear head on or scare yourself to death in the process. EFT can be used to diffuse the frightening emotions and uncomfortable reactions prior to and during a phobic reaction. Exposure to the feared situation needn't be traumatic or a horrendous ordeal. In fact, we do not advise anybody to attempt confronting the object of their fears until they can vividly imagine themselves doing so without any fear response whatsoever. The brain tends to react in the same way towards real and imagined circumstances, so visualizing yourself taking the feared action is a good indication of how you will respond in reality. This is the first stage of EFT phobia treatment.

### peter's story – height phobia

'My phobia was a fear of climbing steps or ladders. Anything over three rungs filled me with fear and dread. I always needed the presence of another person to hold the steps to stop me panicking. The phobia began after I experienced a near fatal accident at work some 25 years ago. The ladder on which I had been standing slipped. I was about 20 feet above a large dangerous machine. To fall onto the machine would have been certain death. I hung on and yelled for help. Being

Sunday there were only a few workers present and no one heard my cries for help. After what seemed a lifetime, my mate did hear and came rushing to help. He rescued me just in time. I had not told anyone the whole story before, because of the painful memories it brought. It must have taken only 20 minutes of EFT to neutralize this emotional event and as a result I have overcome my fear of heights. I am now back to normal and very relieved.'

Peter's phobia had a direct cause and it is easy to see how a fear of heights can develop after such an extreme incident. But it is not always that easy to pinpoint the origin of a phobia to a specific time or event. Sometimes particular memories come back to people when they are using the technique, explaining the origins of their phobia, but it is not essential to know where it came from to reap the benefits. Likewise, it makes very little difference how long a phobia has been experienced or how deeply ingrained it is.

The most difficult phobias to treat with Energy Therapies are the ones with the most aspects. The phobias that contain multiple elements that splinter off in different directions contain more aspects to be cleared. These complex phobias can still be neutralized, but it may take a little longer to eradicate all the aspects that trigger a fear response.

Phobias can have really debilitating effects on people's lives, so when they are treated, the relief and freedom gained is dramatic. Aeroplane journeys that were previously unthinkable have been achieved with ease and tranquillity. Exams have been taken calmly and confidently, instead of the examinee being sick with nerves.

Georgie heard about EFT through a friend. She really was so desperate to be free of her problem that she was willing to try anything. Her mother came with her to the session and we could see how concerned she was for her daughter.

### georgie's story – fear of public toilets

For years, Georgie, aged 20, had been very uncomfortable using any toilet other than her own. This had become progressively worse until she could no longer use any other toilet apart from the one at home. When she went to her local pub she would have to come home to use her own lavatory. When at work she would avoid drinking anything, so that she could wait until her six-hour shift was over and use her own toilet. She couldn't stay anywhere or go anywhere that would prevent her from getting back home in time for the call of nature.

Georgie decided to force herself to get well by booking a holiday abroad, but she was growing increasingly worried the closer the holiday came. This was when she decided to seek help. We tapped for one statement that held an emotional charge, *'Even though people might be able to hear me on the lavatory I deeply and completely accept myself.'* She then remembered a time when she was very small. She was on a car journey with her family and they had to stop the car so that she could urinate. Her brothers made her hurry up, while they were walking around stretching their legs. This made her anxious and she couldn't pee. She became more and more upset at their impatience and, unconsciously, the embarrassment of this event had stayed with her to this day. Her problem became more intense the older she got. We tapped for the feelings that she had at the time – the embarrassment and anger at her brother's mockery, and the disrespect. She felt very strongly that her privacy had been violated and this had been extremely humiliating for her.

Previously, Georgie had been unable to link her current problem to anything specific. After clearing some of her intense emotions during the session, she could see the connection between what happened in the past and her current difficulty. Afterwards, Georgie decided that she wanted to put EFT to the test, so we asked her how she would feel about using our lavatory to see if the treatment had worked. She said she would like to and we will never forget the look on her face as she came back downstairs. She looked at her mum and said 'I could go!' Some time later Georgie reported to us on her progress:

'The same week I was able to use the lavatory at my friend's house and visit several pubs after just one session of EFT. I was able to go on holiday to America. I feel much more relaxed about using unfamiliar toilets. I also feel more confident in myself. My life has expanded to such an extent that I can now go away on business trips.'

## TREATING PHOBIAS

- Firstly, identify what triggers your particular phobic response. Spend some time imagining yourself in the presence of the object of your fear. If this makes you feel uncomfortable, there are several techniques you can employ. Remember you do not gain any points for putting yourself through emotional turmoil. You could imagine the situation on a television screen happening to someone else or at a far distance. This should help to minimize any distress.

- Break the phobia up into the different aspects that frighten you. If it is a fear of spiders, one aspect could be their hairy legs or the way they scurry across the floor, another might be the fear that they will crawl onto you or that you will have to pick one up.
- Write down every aspect that comes to mind. You could include any significant memories that still hold an emotional charge or the words you say to yourself when facing the situation. Write down anything that contributes to the fear, such as the name, the look or physical sensation you experience while in its presence.
- Make sure you grade your overall phobia, as well as each individual aspect so that you can measure your progress.
- Take each aspect in turn and create a statement that describes your reaction specifically. For example:

'Even though I freak out when I see a spider I deeply and completely accept myself.'
'Even though I don't like the way they move I deeply and completely accept myself.'

'Even though I get shivers down my spine when I see a spider I deeply and completely accept myself.'

'Even though I want to run away I deeply and completely accept myself.'

'Even though the look of a spider is revolting I deeply and completely accept myself.'

'Even though seeing other people pick up a spider frightens the living daylights out of me I deeply and completely accept myself.'

'Even though I am terrified that a spider is going to crawl on me I deeply and completely accept myself.'

- Perform a tapping round for each aspect and as many complete rounds for the *remaining* feelings, until each aspect registers a zero.
- Re-imagine the situation that causes you distress and grade your reaction. There should be a noticeable difference. *Check that you have not switched to another aspect of the fear. Or are you now thinking about what would happen if you found a spider in the room?*
- Continue to apply EFT to all the different aspects of the phobia. Once you have successfully neutralized all the frightening aspects, you should be able to imagine yourself calmly confronting the same situation that previously caused anxiety.

Take this process gradually. You don't have to rush into confronting your phobia until you feel comfortable with every aspect of it.

# CONFRONTING YOUR PHOBIA – THE STEP-BY-STEP APPROACH

If you now feel comfortable with all the aspects of the phobia, when you feel ready it is time to confront your phobia using a gradual step-by-step approach. In the following exercise we'll use the example of a fear of birds or feathers to illustrate how this process works. If you haven't got a friend with a bird in a cage that you can use, you could visualize the process.

Start by eradicating all the feelings and aspects prior to the actual meeting. When you feel totally relaxed about the process, enter the house where the bird is kept.

Gradually move closer, step-by-step, stopping at any time if an emotion or different aspect becomes apparent. Proceed in this manner, one step at a time, tapping all the way. You should feel comfortable at every stage. Don't force yourself or allow yourself to become frightened. Remain where you feel safe and tap for any feelings you experience.

As you release any discomfort, you should feel confident about taking your next step. Stop at any time – there are no rules other than being totally relaxed about each step you take. Do not progress until you feel completely calm or indifferent about the next stage. Remember, this is not an endurance test or supposed to frighten you in any way. EFT uses feeling secure and at ease as a bench mark that you are ready to proceed.

Some people thrive on this method of gradual exposure as it builds their confidence in the technique working. Neutralizing a phobia in this way can take five minutes or five days – it is really up to you to decide the pace you want to go. To illustrate the step-by-step approach further, we'll look at the common fear of going to the dentist.

Picture yourself having to make an appointment with the dentist – what are your thoughts and feelings? The statements you choose may be similar to these:

'Even though I couldn't even make an appointment with the dentist I deeply and completely accept myself.'
'Even though I don't want to get over this fear because then I would have no excuse not to go to the dentist I deeply and completely accept myself.'
'Even though thinking about dentists really frightens me I deeply and completely accept myself.'
'Even though I get this sense of dread when I think of making a dental appointment I deeply and completely accept myself.'

Once each of the initial aspects are cleared, move on to the next part of the experience that causes you to be frightened:

'Even though I hate the smell in the dentist's waiting room I deeply and completely accept myself.'
'Even though I get an anxious feeling in my stomach while I wait my turn I deeply and completely accept myself.'
'Even though I feel sick when my name is called I deeply and completely accept myself.'

Once again, apply EFT to every aspect that causes you distress until you can calmly think about sitting in the dentist's waiting room. Then proceed to the next distressing elements:

'Even though I feel trapped in the chair I deeply and completely accept myself.'
'Even though I don't know what to expect I deeply and completely accept myself.'
'Even though I fear the pain involved in dentistry I deeply and completely accept myself.'
'Even though I am frightened of making a fool of myself I deeply and completely accept myself.'
'Even though I don't like feeling out of control I deeply and completely accept myself.'

Then use statements that cover any other part of the procedure that provokes a fear reaction:

'The sharp tools'
'The injection'
'The scraping sensation'
'The noise of the drill'
'The horrible taste'

When you can no longer find any aspect of the dentist that frightens you, the majority of the work is done. Now go through the whole experience from start to finish to see if there is any emotional response to any part of your *imaginary* dental appointment. Even if there is the slightest reaction, tap it away.

When it comes to putting your progress to the test and arranging a real dentist's appointment, you should feel fine about the prospect. If you find it difficult in any way, then you haven't finished yet! Any emotions that do surface are probably connected to different aspects that you haven't tapped for. Ask yourself a few questions to discover what triggered your response and apply the tapping technique to the new elements. You will know you have had a good result when you can book a consultation without any fear.

# HIDDEN ASPECTS

If your phobia is not responding, or only partial relief is obtained, this can indicate that there are still some aspects to the phobia that have not been addressed. Often talking through your fear with a close friend can help reveal unrecognized aspects to the problem. Remember that you are looking for emotionally charged statements. A colleague of ours who had a particularly intense phobia of spiders was asked to talk in depth about her fear. One of the first statements she made was *'spiders are evil'*. She also mentioned that *'spiders were untrustworthy'* because as she could not see a spider's eyes she did not know which direction they were looking. This made her feel out of control. Feeling out of control was probably a deeper and more fundamental issue for her than just a component of a spider phobia. By voicing her fear, it was possible to discover statements that rang true for her. The most effective statements are the ones that use your own descriptions and terminology.

# CHILDREN AND PHOBIAS

Parents will be delighted to know that children can also be treated for phobias using EFT. Gary Craig devotes an entire section to children's problems on his EFT website. Tapping with your child can be very beneficial. Children find the process fun and are extremely open to the technique. It is not necessary for your child to repeat *'I deeply and completely accept myself'* at the end of every statement. Be creative and let them choose what they would like to say. They could use:

> 'Even though I am frightened of the dark, mummy loves me.'
> 'Even though I don't like worms, I feel really brave.'
> 'Even though I am scared of going to school, I'm OK.'
> 'Even though I am frightened of those boys, I'm a really nice person.'

Ask them about their concerns and what physical sensations they experience and then tap for them. Being able to help your child in this way is priceless.

# Chapter 10

# Addictions

Addictions are very common in today's society. Most of us have been addicted to something at one stage in our lives, whether that is food, alcohol, tobacco, coffee, tea, sugar, recreational or medicinal drugs. It is possible to become addicted to almost anything, not only substances but also gambling, relationships, television and shopping.

In effect, caffeine, tannin, nicotine, alcohol, medication and sugar are all poisons. The 'high' we experience is our body's attempt to metabolize the toxin in question. We use the caffeine boost of a cup of coffee in the mornings to wake us up, and after a stressful day a work, the unwinding effects of alcohol to relax us in the evening. Equally, the soothing effect of smoking a cigarette during a social situation or period of difficultly can help to numb feelings of anxiety.

## THE NATURE OF ADDICTION

An addiction is described as the need for the effect that a substance or activity outside oneself produces. It is also seen as the inability to do without that substance or activity either physically, emotionally or psychologically. If you crave a particular substance or activity and find it difficult to stop, you have become dependent. Since the highs you gain from the addictive behaviour are short lived, the dependency will inevitably increase, leaving you in need of more and more stimulation to sustain that initial high.

However, addiction in itself is not the core problem; it is a symptom or strategy that a person adopts as the solution to a problem. The underlying cause of most addictions is emotional. Addictive behaviour fulfils a role for the person that they feel unable to bring about for themselves. It could be:

- The need for emotional fulfilment.
- A distraction or escape from things that are occurring within their lives.
- Stress relief.
- Avoidance of uncomfortable emotions.
- Altering reality to a 'better' existence.
- Palliation of painful and distressing emotions.

Central to addictive behaviour is some form of emotional unease, restlessness or anxiety that we are trying to tranquillize. It also explains why our use of addictive substances increases when we are subject to stress or when we are going through difficult circumstances. We often eat, drink or drug ourselves to blot out uncomfortable emotions. When a person tries to withdraw from their addictive behaviour, emotions that have been suppressed by the addiction quickly come to the surface. A backlash of tears, anger, anxiety, irritability or fear can all come to the fore. This is what makes breaking the habit so difficult. It also explains why so often we end up switching from one addiction to another. We may successfully give up smoking only to become addicted to sweets, food or coffee.

Even though the long-term consequences of overeating, drinking and smoking can be devastating, people often choose to ignore the negative side effects in favour of the apparent short term benefits. In this way an addiction can rule your life until you face up to addressing the underlying problem that produces addictive behaviour.

# ADDICTIONS AND PSYCHOLOGICAL REVERSAL

Psychological Reversal is nearly always present in addictions. This is why people can have such good intentions but they just can't follow them through. Even after being shown how to eliminate an addictive craving with EFT, people will still smoke, eat or drink – conveniently 'forgetting' to use the technique when the need arises. This form of self-sabotage is a classic indication of Psychological Reversal. The unconscious knows that there is more to gain through keeping the addictive behaviour than there would be by releasing it. Although the trade-off would produce physical benefits, the immediate emotional and psychological gratification is lost.

When you add to this the physical and emotional effort that is required to withdraw from an addiction, you are fighting an uphill battle. That is, until you get your body on your side, remove the Psychological Reversal and learn how to step back from addictive cravings and urges.

# THE LIMITATIONS
## OF WILL-POWER

One of the first strategies that some people employ to rid themselves of addictions is to use will-power to break the chain of events. Yet will-power is designed as a short-term measure and it should only be used in cases of emergency and crisis situations.

Relentlessly using will-power to stop addictive behaviour is exhausting and people often end up exerting their will-power to stop thinking about the very thing they are trying not to think about! The problem here is that there are so many triggers that remind them of what they are missing. Being in a pub environment when you are trying to give up smoking is a prime example. Our friends or partner may smoke and cigarettes are constantly on display or for sale. We see others smoking, we can smell the smoke and see the pleasure that others are having while smoking. All that is needed to bring our will-power tumbling down is a bad day or a slip of concentration. At the time, you may kid yourself 'I just need this one to get me over this' but, inevitably, you are back on the addiction treadmill. This is why people so often resign themselves to being a smoker.

EFT practitioners choose to believe that every person is doing the very best they can at any given moment, given the choices available to them. EFT can enable a person to take back their own self-empowerment. If you feel ready to approach your addictive behaviour, EFT application can help to support that decision. As a technique it can make withdrawal from cigarettes, alcohol and food much easier, quicker and more comfortable. EFT will release the pattern of addiction at an energetic level. It can:

- Help to focus motivation and perseverance to achieve your goal.

emotional healing

- Remove the Psychological Reversed parts of you that will block progress or even prevent you from starting.
- Eradicate the physical cravings as and when they arise.
- Release the emotional contributing factors.
- Offer overall support while going through the process of change.

## ENERGETIC DISRUPTION OF A CRAVING

Every craving starts with a thought and the addictive thought automatically produces a disruption in the body's energy system. This, in turn, is experienced as a physical sensation that we recognize as a craving for a particular substance. If denied, the craving sensation becomes stronger and stronger until the person gives in. As a result an enormous amount of our precious energy becomes tied up in this process.

None of us were born with the need for a cigarette or an addictive behaviour. We have come to look forward to the pleasurable feelings that we associate with the addictive behaviour. Before this we relied on other internal strategies and strengths to achieve inner peace and through EFT you can return to this inner balance. It can also be used to diminish uncomfortable feelings that underlie or arise when withdrawing from addictive behaviour. Addictive urges can literally be stopped in their tracks.

## lucy's story – cigarette addiction

Lucy came to see us with a shopping list of emotional problems and painful memories and these were all cleared very quickly. As Lucy was putting on her coat, Paul mentioned how effective EFT was with addictions. He told her how he had managed to stop smoking by accidentally neutralizing his own cravings while working with a client with a smoking addiction. Lucy said that she wanted to quit so, never missing an opportunity, Paul tapped away her current craving for a cigarette. This impromptu session took less than five minutes to complete. Here is Lucy's own account of what happened.

'After my EFT session with Paul, we got onto the subject of addictions and I asked him if EFT could be used to stop smoking. I hadn't intended to stop right there and then. I meant that I wanted to stop smoking at some point in the future.

'He asked how much I wanted a cigarette out of ten and I replied that it felt like eight out of ten. The EFT was applied a couple of times and I no longer wanted a cigarette. My desire just faded away. Paul explained that the craving may return and that it would be my choice whether I had a cigarette or tapped for the craving. I thanked him and left. When I got to my car I saw an unopened packet of cigarettes in the glove compartment, but I felt no inclination to have one. I still didn't want one when waiting at the railway crossing. Later that night, my partner upset me – when this happens I would normally go outside the back door for a cigarette – but I still didn't feel the need.

'After a few days I put the same cigarette packet back in the car, as I had been carrying them around with me everywhere I went – just in case. It is almost as if I can't remember why I smoked or what it was like. The most amazing thing is that there were no withdrawal symptoms. I didn't have any bouts of bad temper; I forgot the habits that were associated with smoking. The other important thing is that the triggers that would normally start off a craving didn't affect me this time. After 30 years of smoking 20 cigarettes a day – it is just incredible – I am now a non-smoker.'

# DEALING WITH ADDICTIONS

## Preparing for Release

If you are serious about releasing your addiction some background work can be very helpful to uncover powerful Set-Up statements that will realign your energy system. Make sure that you do not attempt to withdraw from any serious drug problem or medication without first enlisting medical supervision.

Most addicts will say that they like their addiction because it is fun or enjoyable. But why do they need to take a substance to have fun? Others will say 'It relaxes me' and this begs the question 'Why are you not relaxed already?' Finding out exactly what purpose your addictive behaviour holds for you is the first step to diminishing its hold.

## Be Curious

Set aside some quiet time and as much paper as you need. Explore the following questions to help you begin. Once you have managed to find your own answers, write down all the thoughts and feelings you have about your addiction. Try not to judge yourself, just observe what your fears and anxieties are.

- When did the addiction start?
- Why did it continue?
- What need does it fulfil in you?
- What does the addiction stop you from feeling?
- What times are you particularly drawn to doing it?
- What are the triggers in your day that encourage your addiction?
- How would you feel without the addictive substance or behaviour?
- What positive feelings and negative feelings do you have about stopping?

Once you have discovered more about your addiction, read what you have written, this time underlining any significant words or sentences that could be used as personal Set-up statements. Then apply EFT in the usual way to as many of them as you need. For instance:

'Even though I enjoy smoking/drinking/bingeing …
'Even though I don't want to give up …
'Even though It relaxes me …
'Even though I like the sensation …
'Even though I would feel deprived without it …
'Even though I'm too weak to give-up …
'Even though I have always been a smoker …

... I deeply and completely accept myself.'

## The Pros and Cons of Giving Up

To gain insight into any Psychological Reversal that may impede your progress get another piece of paper and draw a set of scales. Place all your positive reasons for stopping the addiction on one side and all the reasons and excuses not to on the other. In order to be successful the scales need to be weighted in the right direction. (see Fig. 18, page 83) If you discover more reasons 'not to' than benefits, applying EFT to the negative points can tip the balance in your favour.

'Even though I really don't want to give up smoking I deeply and completely accept myself.'
'Even though I can't get myself together to give up drinking I deeply and completely accept myself.'
'Even though life would be empty without this I deeply and completely accept myself.'

## Eradicating Cravings

Performing the preparation work beforehand will place you in a very strong position. Once you feel ready to begin the process of stopping, your next step is to learn how to eradicate the cravings that are likely to surface. You may like to use the technique prior to actually giving up to minimize your current intake and to build your confidence in the technique. Each time an addictive urge is experienced, ask yourself:

- Why do I want the desired object?
- What am I currently feeling emotionally and physically?
- Where am I when the craving hits?
- What has just happened?
- How would the substance make me feel if I were to partake?
- Am I attempting to avoid or produce a certain feeling?

From your answers you will be able to identify personal triggers that can be tapped for each time a craving is experienced. Additionally, it allows you to be forewarned of vulnerable times when more tapping would be beneficial.

'Even though I feel really anxious and want to raid the fridge I deeply and completely accept myself.'
'Even though I have this physical craving sensation I deeply and completely accept myself.'
'Even though every time I feel unable to relax I reach for a drink I deeply and completely accept myself.'

After working out your craving patterns, you may like to start working with the actual substance or activity. If the addiction in question is a substance, having the substance present produces a powerful focus, although you can be just as successful by vividly imagining the situation. The technique also works better if you wait until you are actually experiencing a craving that you can score. Measure your level of desire or craving out of ten. Tap throughout the session for any emotional, physical or psychological need that arises:

emotional healing

- Look at the substance in front of you.
- Smell it.
- Taste a little of it.
- Pick it up and hold it in your free hand.

You could use statements such as:

> 'Even though I love the taste of wine I deeply and completely accept myself.'
> 'Even though I really want that piece of chocolate cake/a cigarette I deeply and completely accept myself.'

If you have carried out this part of the procedure correctly you should observe a significant drop in the level of your craving. It is quite common for the desire for a cigarette to fall from ten to zero within a few minutes. This can be repeated every time you want a cigarette. Most people report that originally they were desperate for a cigarette or a bar of chocolate, but after the tapping they can take it or leave it, they are no longer bothered. This is what happens naturally when you remove the emotional charge and energetic disruption behind a craving. The substance becomes neutral.

After a while it is likely that the craving will return. If and when it does, just repeat the tapping for the craving until it diminishes entirely. Tap every time you think about the substance or when you find yourself in a situation in which you would normally partake in the addictive behaviour. Remember that this approach is not about using will-power, although you do have to remember to tap whenever you feel a strong desire. Psychological Reversal is often the reason that addictive urges return. This is why it can be useful to design a daily schedule of tapping. Tap up to 25 times a day if you need to. This will enable the reversed energy flow to be corrected at regular intervals and help to reduce cravings before they occur. It also helps to design a weekly review to monitor your progress. This will prevent addictive behaviour being transferred to other substances when the root cause has not yet been addressed and it helps you to target any specific problematic areas.

Bringing the body back into balance will reduce unhealthy addictions and help you to feel calmer and less anxious. As the days go by, the need for tapping will become less and less. If you are really ready to be done with your addiction EFT can be your greatest ally. Good luck.

## Chapter 11

# Physical Complaints

Just as sufficient blood supply is vital to physical health, so is balanced energy flow. Meridians allow energy to travel throughout the body, nourishing and strengthening all the organs and physical processes. The energy system is the connecting framework between the mind and the body. A disrupted energy system will inevitably lead to problems and imbalances within the body. Recurring disruption within the meridians can lead to chronic physical complaints and health problems. Initially, disorder begins within the energy system. Balancing the disrupted energy patterns allows the body to heal.

## THE BODY–MIND CONNECTION

In the West we have been educated to view illness as an exclusively biological process of disorder, infection or malfunction. This view of illness implies that individuals have no control over their own biological processes. If this was true, who or what *is* in control of our physical biology?

The suggestion that illness could have its roots in the mind has often been disregarded in the past. Yet, as increasing evidence is gathered, the body–mind connection is becoming more readily accepted. The holistic professions view physical illness and the resulting changes in biology as the direct result of dis-ease within the mental, emotional and energetic levels of a person. Since every emotion we experience produces a release of hormones into the bloodstream, our thoughts and feelings continually influence our body. Repressed feelings and emotional baggage are all seen as fundamental factors that can cause the deterioration of health. Pent-up emotions, such as fear, negativity and stress, can be as detrimental to our physical well-being as they are to our emotional happiness. You can do as much damage to yourself by ignoring unexpressed feelings as you can by ignoring a physical symptom. Worry, anxiety and stress also do a great deal of harm to our physical well-being and are at the root of countless health problems.

EFT will not mask important symptoms that require medical attention or suppress illness to a deeper level. However, before applying the technique to a health condition you need to take responsibility for your own well-being. It is advisable to seek medical advice and diagnosis before administering EFT for physical complaints.

Regardless of the health problem, EFT should help at least to an extent. On the spot relief can be obtained from all manner of acute physical ailments such as

allergic reactions
asthmatic breathing
bee stings
bloating
coughs
earache
faintness
fatigue

hangovers
hay fever
headaches
hot flushes
indigestion
influenza
jet lag
morning sickness

| | |
|---|---|
| muscle tension | stomach upsets |
| nasal congestions | sunburn |
| nausea | toothache |
| sneezing fits | |

as well as chronic conditions such as:

| | |
|---|---|
| allergies | nervous bowel conditions |
| arthritis | pain and neuralgia |
| back pain | postviral fatigue syndrome |
| chronic fatigue | pre-menstrual syndrome |
| circulation problems | Raynaud's disease |
| constipation | sinusitis |
| frozen shoulders | tendonitis |
| impotence | tennis elbow |
| insomnia | tremors |
| joint stiffness | underactive thyroid conditions |

Many people have gained relief from the symptoms of physical illness where other treatments have failed, including conditions that have resulted from mechanical damage. Even if you think that EFT couldn't possibly be of help, there is nothing more than a few minutes to lose and everything to gain.

Jenny used EFT for various issues that had been plaguing her, but she hadn't thought of applying it to her PMS. After trying it, she rang us to describe the success she had.

### jenny's story – pre-menstrual syndrome

'EFT has helped me with so many problems and the biggest difference has been with my hormones and monthly cycle. Before EFT, I experienced irregular and flooding periods for many years. When my period was due it would ruin a week and a half out of every month and the pain was diabolical – out of this world. Now it only niggles. I had tried all sorts of treatments without success. Now, for the first time in my life, my periods are lighter and I don't get so moody the week before. My partner used to dread my moods, but now he doesn't even know when I am due to have a period. Now if I have any worrying discomfort or emotion, I just tap away.'

# DEALING
## WITH PHYSICAL
# COMPLAINTS

The basic technique remains the same, although the approach is slightly different. The treatment needs to be applied regularly to achieve results, preferably several times a day. It can take time for physical healing to occur, since tissue may need to regenerate, deposits may need to be re-absorbed and lesions repaired, before relief is achieved. However, after a while the energy system will become sufficiently re-organised to sustain the changes and will produce a more balanced energy flow.

If you are treating an ongoing health complaint, flare-ups should occur less frequently as time goes on. Chronic problems tend to weaken in response to regular tapping. There are people who have persistently applied the technique over a three-month period who have reaped enormous benefits from daily applications.

Mavis wrote to us to share her EFT experience with migraine headaches, which she had suffered for nearly 10 years.

### mavis's story – migraine headaches

Mavis was at her wits' end. She had tried everything known to her, but was still suffering from a migraine attack approximately every three weeks. The symptoms included severe pain, vomiting, blurred vision and disorientation. After being taught how to use EFT, she started working on her migraines straight away. We didn't hear anything from her until three months later, when she wrote to us. Here is what she had to say.

'I am pleased to report that my migraines have stopped. I wanted to leave some time before writing to you in case I got the dreaded headache – I have given it every chance to manifest and on a few occasions I've even dared it! At first I just got the symptoms that came prior to a migraine, such as the aching eyes and disorientation, but no pain or vomiting, which meant I could carry on with a normal day and use the tapping technique.

'It took a while to realize how much these migraine attacks ruled my life and what I unconsciously did to avoid situations which might bring one on. And then, to realize that it was no longer necessary to do so, what freedom!'

Mavis's migraines responded in a typical way to EFT. Addressed symptom by symptom, the hold the migraines had over her started to loosen immediately. Then only the initial symptoms appeared. Mavis applied EFT straight away when these telltale signs appeared and saved herself from the ensuing headache. After a few weeks of tapping the whole condition disappeared.

# CHASING
## THE PAIN

Just as emotional issues tend to change focus and contain different aspects, physical complaints appear to follow a similar pattern. As you start working with the problem, they are quite likely to change nature, sensation or location. We call this 'chasing the pain' and it is an indication that the physical complaint is subsiding. For instance, you may start by treating a stiff pain in your neck which, once cleared, leaves you with an aching sensation in your arm. You address the aching arm only to find that now you have a sharp pain in your shoulder. This is a natural occurrence resulting from blocked energy working its way through the meridian system. After a few minutes of tapping the whole condition should cease, leaving you free of pain.

There is a good possibility that the discomfort might return at some later stage, especially if you suffer from a chronic illness or degenerative condition that requires medication on a regular basis. This is because we all have certain physical weaknesses and susceptibilities. However, if it does return, re-apply the technique as and when necessary.

When addressing a physical condition, the Set-Up statement needs to include a specific description of the feeling or physical sensation of distress. For example:

> '*Throbbing* headache'
> '*Stiffness* in my neck'
> '*Dragging* pain'
> '*Sore* pain in my throat'
> '*Pins and needles* in my feet'

If you name the symptoms you experience, it often produces better results than if you just name the medical condition. Identify the problem you wish to address and assign a score relating to the level of physical discomfort out of ten. Each symptom is then treated as a separate aspect. Apply EFT to each symptom, using a statement that defines the feeling of discomfort or pain, for example:

'Even though I have this piercing pain in my eye I deeply and completely accept myself.'

followed by a reminder phrase of:

'This *piercing* pain in my eye'

Re-check the level of discomfort and apply an additional round for the remaining pain if necessary:

'Even though I still have some remaining piercing pain in my eye I deeply and completely accept myself.'

Use a reminder phrase that includes the word *remaining*:

'This *remaining* piercing pain in my eye'

Continue until the discomfort has subsided.

# EMOTIONAL
## FACTORS

Another successful way of treating physical complaints is to find out whether there are any emotions that are contributing to the condition. The flow of energy throughout the system can be interrupted by emotional problems and often the body will express emotions that we feel unable or unwilling to express. The symptoms of illness often reflect our internal feelings. So, stiffness in the body can often indicate rigidity within attitude and outlook. Relationship difficulties can manifest as physical problems in the reproductive organs and so on. Addressing the psychological aspects that lie behind a dis-ease can remove the imbalance that leads to the creation of physical illness.

The language we use to describe our ailment can also hold vital clues. *'This job is breaking my back', 'I can't stomach it anymore', 'He's a pain in the neck', 'I feel suffocated'.* Not only does our language illustrate which areas of life are causing stress, but sometimes we use exactly the same words to describe our physical complaint. These also make excellent opening statements, combining both physical and emotional issues of a problem at the same time.

The sensation of physical discomfort that we experience can indicate possible underlying emotional contributors. *'Weeping* wounds', *'Nagging* pains', *'Angry* sores', *'Numb* body parts' are all prime examples of the body acting as an overflow for a person's emotional state. Illness and physical symptoms can often be approached in more than one way. At times, tapping for physical symptoms can bring contributing emotional factors or memories into your awareness. If this happens, targeting the emotion specifically will be extremely beneficial. At other times, physical problems can spontaneously disappear after tapping for emotional issues.

### anita's story – spondylitis: past emotional wounds

Anita had experienced severe pain in her neck, shoulders and head for over 20 years. Her consultant diagnosed spondylitis. Over the years she had exhausted both orthodox and complementary approaches in attempts to relieve her painful problems and nothing seemed to work for more than a few days. During her EFT session with Val she tuned into the physical pain and her thoughts drifted back to the time when her previous husband had an affair that eventually destroyed their marriage. She tells her story:

'I saw all of our faces, my husband's, the "girl's" and my sad one. My husband told me that there was nothing in their friendship. The girl had been unhappy at home and needed someone to talk to. I was asked to befriend her as well! I did this for a while, but intuitively I knew their relationship was more than they would admit to.

'Although I still had grave doubts and uncertainties about our relationship, I wanted to start a family. The child issue was always avoided. He told me that he needed me to continue at work to help with the finances. So I put all my efforts into my teaching career.

'The crunch came 18 months later when I found out that she had told him that if we ever had a child she would leave him. I was furious and appalled that her feelings were more precious than mine. I was also angry that I had been kept in the dark, lied to, and led to believe my imagination was running riot. No wonder he avoided the subject of children!

'I told him to leave and then discovered he already had a flat to run to. I was furious, but mostly depressed. I was so overwhelmed with feelings of rejection, hurt, anger and grief. My faith in human nature had gone. The sadness was over-whelming as I realized he didn't care what he lost financially. This proved his love for her, not me. Shortly after the swift divorce, they had the child I so desperately wanted.

'A few years later I was granted a good and loving relationship and given a beautiful child. Val and I worked through the hurt, depression and sadness. But the most intense emotion was the suppressed anger. I was furious at the deceit and I was so cross and angry with myself for being so foolish. At last I was able to release all those pent up emotions. A feeling of peace and contentment flowed over me. I shouted aloud "They're gone!" My neck and shoulders no longer torment me. I feel normal again I am free of pain at last.'

Anita's painful emotions were trapped within her body. Neck problems can often relate to experiences in the past that we do not want to look at. The body appears to reflect our emotional state, by physically making it 'painful' to 'look behind' us. Releasing the backlog of unexpressed feelings frees the energy system from emotional interference.

If you suspect that emotional issues are contributing to your physical ailment 'The Colour of Pain' exercise can be a very useful technique.

# THE COLOUR
## OF PAIN

This exercise is designed to uncover any emotional component that may be contributing to a physical illness. Spend some time relaxing in a peaceful environment. With your eyes closed move your awareness to the core of your physical complaint.

- If it had a colour what would it be?
- How big a surface area does it cover? Is it larger or smaller than your hand?
- Is it moving or still?
- Is it solid or transparent?
- How old is it? (Accept the first answer that comes to mind.)
- When did it begin?
- What events led up to it?
- If it had an emotion or feeling what would it be? (If you cannot obtain a clear answer ask yourself, 'If I had to guess, what would it be?')
- If you were suddenly healthy right now what possible benefits would you gain? What things might it mean you would 'have to' do, or would 'lose out' on?

Apply EFT to any emotions or descriptions that you uncovered. Afterwards, look again at the internal complaint – often the colour will change from a dark colour to a lighter colour. The energy may move rather than remain stuck. The problem may be replaced by an image that is more healthy or positive.

Even injuries or conditions that have been caused by physical damage can be helped by this technique.

### veronica's story – acute back pain

While bending over, Veronica pulled a muscle in her back. She experienced the usual pain and discomfort associated with this condition. Having suffered from a bad back on and off for the last 25 years, she knew that she would be in pain for at least the next few weeks. Three weeks later she was still suffering, but refusing to give-in. She went shopping for the weekly supplies; this was a big mistake, the pain was excru- ciating and she didn't know what she wanted to do most – cry or abandon the trolley. On returning, Veronica decided to try EFT to see if it could help in anyway.

Although she didn't really believe that EFT would help with back pain, she was desperate. She told us how she applied it to various aspects of her physical pain, but she hadn't gained any relief. It wasn't until she said each statement with real conviction that she started to make progress. After complet- ing several tapping rounds she realized that the pain had gone and she felt much more comfortable. Veronica still needed to respect the fact that her back needed time to heal and so she took things very easy over the next few days. She concluded by saying, 'My recovery was so much quicker than normal, the tapping really did speed up the healing process.'

# PHYSICAL COMPLAINTS AND PSYCHOLOGICAL REVERSAL

Health problems can have both positive and negative effect upon us. A sudden illness can give us the excuse we need to avoid a difficult situation or stressful occasion. Ill health can also be a feedback mechanism that stops us from pushing ourselves into exhaustion. It can give us the time and space we need for reflection and to develop self-awareness. Most importantly, it can draw our attention to unexpressed emotions that need to be cleared in order for us to be happy and healthy.

Psychological Reversal is very common in physical health problems and it plays a vital part in all degenerative and chronic conditions. The reversed energy flow literally keeps the condition in place. Auto-immune diseases are a prime example of the body being at odds with itself.

Illness can hold secondary gains just as any other condition. A physical complaint can enable you to off-load responsibility, avoid work or gain attention from others. It may suit part of you to feel 'pitied' or be thought of as a 'martyr'. Ill health can hide a fear of failure, feelings of inadequacy or low self-esteem. Disease can often disguise more fundamental issues that we have not (or do not want to) acknowledge about ourselves.

Psychological Reversal is not a conscious flaw or weakness, it is an unconscious process. Left unchecked, these chronic reversals of energy flow manifest in a malfunctioning body. As long as Psychological Reversal is present, it is very difficult to gain any relief.

EFT can be a great comfort for physical aspects of illness. It can be applied to the negative feelings that accompany, or are created in response to poor health. Post-operatively, it can be used for the anxiety and nerves that people experience, helping to keep an individual calm and relaxed during a very stressful time. EFT has the ability to speed up recovery time and help with pain relief. It is a subtle, yet powerful tool that can enhance the healing capacities that are innate within us and offer crucial support in any healing process.

# Chapter 12

# Beliefs

A significant discovery highlighted by EFT is that our thoughts produce energy. Every thought we experience, positive or negative, has an influence on our entire energy system. This is why it is essential that the quality of our thoughts is as positive and life-affirming as possible. This has never been more apparent than with our beliefs.

Have you ever wondered why things go wrong in your life? Why you attract the experiences that you do? Why you repeatedly have similar feelings of inadequacy or low self-esteem? And what exactly does determine whether you succeed or fail? If you are manifesting difficulties in your life or are unable to attract what you desire, it could be time to examine your beliefs.

Our beliefs are one of the most fundamental and defining factors shaping our behaviour and our experience of the world. We all have beliefs. We have beliefs about money, relationships, sex, work, the correct way to do things and, most importantly, about ourselves. We have beliefs about our capabilities, our potential, our social standing and what we can expect for ourselves. Our list of beliefs is seemingly endless.

# POSITIVE AND NEGATIVE BELIEFS

What you believe affects your behaviour in a very direct way. Not feeling 'good enough' will prevent you from taking opportunities that may prove you right. Any situation that challenges your basic worth will feel scary and too much of a risk.

Your basic beliefs can stop you from doing so many things. For instance, maybe you would like to change your job. You may see a vacancy advertised in the paper and think to yourself *'I would really like this job, it's all that I've ever asked for, it's perfect'.* But then up pops a voice that says *'Don't be silly, you can't do that, you're not good enough'.* The inner voice goes on to say *'You might have to give reports at meetings'* which promptly reminds you that you always turn red when reading in front of others – not to mention the stuttering! So by the end of your internal conversation, you decide not to apply for the job. This makes you feel even worse about yourself and adds another compounding experience to your already powerful belief that you will *'never be good enough'.*

If you had positive self-belief, you would apply for the job quite happily. There would be no little voice putting you down or convincing you that you would fail. Even if you didn't get offered the job, it wouldn't be the end of the world – your basic self-worth would still remain intact. Beliefs can either help or hinder us. We have both positive and negative beliefs. Positive beliefs support us and encourage us to 'have a go', the negative ones paralyse and stop us dead in our tracks.

Weeding out beliefs that have a negative influence creates new future possibilities. Once a belief is formed, we set about proving ourselves right and often we find just what we are looking for! For instance, if you believe that all men are philanderers, the chances are that you will attract every philanderer in the vicinity. They may appear different, look entirely different, have different jobs, come from different backgrounds, but in the end they will all cheat on you somehow. This is not a conscious intention on your part, but an old belief pattern that is running the show. On the other hand, if you believe that all men are supportive, the men you attract into your life will tend to be supportive.

## MAKE BELIEVE

Once a belief is created we attract experiences that fit within our belief system and repel events that fall outside our model of the world. In essence, we create our own version of reality. This can be very hard to see at first, as our friends will share similar core beliefs. This is because we are more likely to choose friends who hold matching values and beliefs than people who don't. We then have a mutual '*how life is*' understanding with those closest and most influential in our lives. Anyone with extremely different beliefs will create conflict and is unlikely to be attracted to you. Our friends will tend to share the same principles in life and each social group will have a code of ethics of their own. Examples of the common bonds that link certain people include:

- Nail them before they nail you!
- Money and success are the most important things in life.
- Don't expect too much from life.
- Work hard.

- Play hard.
- Be happy with your lot.
- Always strive to improve yourself.

Each person acts and interprets their life experiences in their individual fashion and will accrue events that verify their beliefs and disregard experiences that fall outside them. Together we create a communal view of reality that feels comfortable.

As a result, life experiences tend to fit our internal model of 'who we are'. Expanding our comfort zone to include a larger version of our own potential can feel wrong, as if it doesn't apply to us. If you believe that you're a failure, that belief will colour all your experiences. Events that would be perceived differently by others will often bring you back to the same conclusion – that you're a failure. Relationship break-ups, redundancy, financial problems will all be viewed through the same filter. Regardless of what actually happens, the individual who believes they are a failure will become the architect of their own disaster. Removing the limiting belief would enable them to view their circumstances from a more balanced perspective, incorporating all the unique elements and contributing factors that went into the previous experiences.

Making the connection between your internal thought processes and your external circumstances is a huge step toward breaking through the psychological patterns that influence your life. Frequently, we ignore our inner thoughts and forget to challenge beliefs that are no longer appropriate and often what we believe about ourselves feels unchangeable. Until our hidden beliefs are brought into our conscious awareness, challenged and re-thought, they will remain intact. Val uncovered a belief that was still present after 40 years. It is a prime example of belief formation.

### val's story – 'stupid' belief

'I always had a belief that I was stupid and not good enough. When asking for help I would feel a nuisance and expect people to get angry with me. I started to use EFT on this belief and it lead me to some surprising memories from my early school days, which I hated and tried to forget. But now it felt important to remember why.

'I enjoyed my first school year and liked my teacher because she was kind, gentle and always explained things patiently. I did not like the next teacher; she was impatient and had a hard face. I knew she had upset me, but could not remember why, so I tapped for *"Even though I can't remember how she upset me I deeply and completely accept myself."* Then memories started to come back to me; I remembered asking several times if she would explain something to me that I did not understand. She became angry and shouted at me, calling me "stupid" and to stop being a nuisance. I felt so hurt and embarrassed that I wanted to hide, but there was nowhere to go so I withdrew inside myself and pretended it did not matter. After this, I always hid at the back of the class and I never spoke out even when I knew the answer to a question.

'I recalled that throughout my secondary school years I never tried in class, as there was this ever-present belief that I couldn't do anything because I was stupid and not good enough. When the time came for me to leave school and look for work I overheard two teachers talking about a job vacancy at our local bank. One of them said 'Valerie isn't good enough to work there' and of course this just reinforced my feelings of inadequacy.

'I tapped for all of the painful memories that surfaced, I felt lighter, stronger and more confident after each round of EFT. These horrible experiences simply didn't matter anymore. I now teach EFT, hold spiritual discovery groups and run work-shops at the Eastbourne College of Arts and Technology. If only my teachers could see me now.'

Most of us have some beliefs that were formed in school that prevent us from being so much more than our beliefs allow. But it is sometimes our beliefs that are stupid, not us. Frequently, the belief we hold about ourselves actually belongs to someone else. It can be hard to distinguish between your own beliefs and those that have been passed on by another.

# CHILDHOOD
# BELIEFS

Clearly, our family beliefs are the most integral and ingrained of all. Our parents are important teachers and how they interacted with each other and with you as a child will have a lasting effect on all your subsequent relation-ships. How they spoke to each other, expressed their emotions, handled difficulties, disciplined, laughed, cried, worked and the nature of their politi-cal views will all play a part in establishing your belief system. Was there plenty to go round or never enough? What did your parents teach you about life? Remember, it's quite possible that your parents' beliefs may not be their own. Their beliefs could have been passed down from their parents and maybe from generations beyond that.

Beliefs are often formed in early childhood and not questioned when we reach adulthood. When we explore the origins of our beliefs, they sometimes come from painful memories or experiences in the past. They are the result of our schoolteachers, classmates, bullies, first romantic relationships, films we have watched, books we have read, in fact the whole of our society. If something unpleasant happens to us once, we may not take too much notice, twice and it gets our attention, three times and it becomes an undeniable truth! To prevent ourselves from being hurt we form a protective mechanism against it happening again and a belief is formed.

- If you cry you get laughed at.
- It's not safe to express anger.
- I need to be good in order to be loved.

This is how we learn and attempt to avoid pain and suffering in the future. But, childhood experiences are *childhood* experiences, they do not need to colour every other experience after that. As adults, we develop skills to help us navigate through our emotional worlds. We learn to understand ourselves and others better.

Our beliefs, if appropriate, are meant to serve us, act as guidelines, keep us from making the same mistakes again. However, the beliefs that underpin most of our experiences were created within a child's mind and some of them were formed as a result of a traumatic incident or unfortunate circumstances. Rather than keep us safe, our beliefs can instead hold us prisoner.

Anna had a problem she wanted to address that she felt connected to her beliefs.

### anna's story – over-responsibility

'I had taken responsibility too seriously and could not understand where it had come from. I thought that maybe EFT would enable me to gain some insight into the problem.

I started with the opening statement *"Even though I don't understand why I take responsibility so seriously I deeply and completely accept myself."* As I did this, my thoughts suddenly went back to childhood. I was about nine years old and was at junior school. I volunteered to be a school monitor as I enjoyed the responsibility. I was soon the cloakroom, playground, blackboard, register and even toilet monitor and I loved it.

'The school had very strict policies and at lunchtime we had to sit quietly and eat our dinner. During lunchtime one day, I was giggling with my friend and the teacher caught me. As I returned to the classroom the teacher ordered me out to the front. She informed the whole class that I had been laughing at her during lunch break and was therefore not a very responsible child. I was told that due to my "irresponsibility" I could not be trusted, so all my monitor duties were taken away.

'I had not realized what a lasting effect this incident had on me. It became clear that I had formed the belief that "laughter causes things to be taken away from you". As a result I had become very serious with regard to any responsibility. In fact, I had become over-responsible.

'I tapped for all the issues surrounding the past incident. I have found myself more relaxed around responsibility ever since the EFT session. It is safe for me to laugh again.'

What we believe, we experience and what we experience is the story of our lives. The outside world is a reflection of our internal world. If you don't know what your beliefs are, the quickest way of discovering what you are thinking is external feedback from your life experience.

- If you don't respect yourself, others will not respect you either.
- If you don't listen to yourself, no-one will listen to you.
- If you treat yourself like a doormat so will others.
- If you feel inferior others will tend to treat you so.

And equally:

- If you love yourself, others will love you in return.
- If you feel worthy, others will find you worth knowing.
- If you honour your own talents others will recognize you.

If you want a new relationship, a different job, a pay rise or more respect from your colleagues, it is time to clear out any negative beliefs that may be preventing you from achieving what you desire.

One way to identify your beliefs is to look at your past, paying particular attention to the significant positive and negative events that you have experienced. As you review each situation, ask yourself what someone who attracted that experience would have to believe? Then ask yourself if this is true for you.

# THE BRIDGE
## OF BELIEFS

In a moment, close your eyes and prepare to relax.

**1** See your dream or ambition in the distance. You are standing on one side of a bridge and your dream or ambition is on the other side. It could be passing a test, finding a loving relationship, running a successful business – or anything else you choose.

**2** See a picture of what it would look like just on the other side of the bridge. Remember to include all the important details and make it as real as possible. If it is a dream house, for example, see all the qualities that are important to you, right down to the welcome mat in the entrance hall.

**3** When you have filled in as many details and made the picture as vivid as possible, you are ready to take your first step. This bridge is only strong enough to support you. It will not take the weight of any negative beliefs that are in conflict with your desire. What negative beliefs about yourself or your life would stop you from reaching the other side and realizing your dreams? You may be surprised by what memories flash up for you. Each negative belief needs to be tapped away before you decide to believe in yourself and do what is practical and necessary to have your dreams come true.

The Bridge of Beliefs exercise helps you focus on what you want and iden-tify the limiting beliefs that are holding you back. All the positive affirmations in the world will be ineffective if you have an underlying restrictive belief. Gary Craig calls this kind of belief a 'tail-ender'. Tail-enders are the little voices that pipe up after you have stated what you want. You could repeat *'I am now successful'* 50 times a day, only to have a negative tail-ender saying *'but, my father always said you have to earn success and I'm no good at anything, so how can I earn it?'* attach itself to the affirmation. A tail-ender is like the bottom line of what you really think about yourself. It represents a tiny voice inside you whispering *'But I'd feel a fraud'*, *'Things like that just don't happen for me'* or *'Things always go wrong'*.

In order for affirmations and all kinds of positive thinking to be successful, conflicting negative beliefs need to be cleared. Once all the barriers have been removed, achieving your goal will be much easier.

## FINDING YOUR RESTRICTING BELIEFS

To establish if you have any restricting beliefs, carry out the following exer-cise. After reading the list of headings, complete each sentence. You may have to be very quick to catch a core belief, as they tend to flit in and out of our awareness very quickly. Usually the very first answer that you receive is the right one. Ask yourself:

- 'What do I believe about myself, in relation to … ?'
- Money
- Relationships

- Career
- Marriage
- Health
- Sex
- Happiness

If you reveal any unhealthy beliefs, apply EFT straight away. Use the VOC scale described earlier (*see* page 92), to rate your level of belief in each statement. Once you have an approximate score, start tapping for any beliefs that are standing in the way of accomplishing what you desire. For example:

'Even though I believe I will always end up on my own I deeply and completely accept myself.'
'Even though I believe I will never find happiness I deeply and completely accept myself.'
'Even though I believe it isn't safe to express my feelings I deeply and completely accept myself.'
'Even though I believe I am inadequate I deeply and completely accept myself.'

Keep tapping until you feel totally detached from the statement. Bring your level of belief down to zero. Once you stop believing something it ceases to be true for you and you become open to attracting new and exciting experiences. You will probably find that the most difficult area of your life is the very area that contains limiting beliefs. Clearing out these old beliefs makes way for new and positive future possibilities to occur.

## Chapter 13

# Weight Loss

Weight can be a very emotive issue. Our feelings surrounding our physical shape and appearance can be very intense. Being overweight can produce a wide range of distressing emotions including despair, self-hate, frustration, guilt, obsession, not to mention feelings of helplessness and being out of control. Being overweight is as much a psychological issue as it is physical. Once again, the weight itself is not the problem; it is only a symptom. The cause lies elsewhere and the reason for many weight problems is an emotional one.

Using EFT for weight loss is very different to other methods. It involves getting your energy moving, but not necessarily through physical activity. Excess weight can be caused by energetic imbalances and blockages as much as physical factors. This approach concentrates on reducing the energetic blocks to losing weight and balancing the unhealthy eating patterns, cravings and resistance to losing weight. If you are serious about losing excess pounds, daily tapping will help immensely.

# OVERWEIGHT AND
## EMOTIONAL ISSUES

Food represents many things, including love, security, pleasure and gratification, and for most of us eating is a pleasurable experience. However, at times the food we place in our mouths is 'feeding' other parts of us. Food can be used to fill an emotional vacuum, such as loneliness and boredom, or it can be used to push down other uncomfortable feelings that we are trying to avoid. Our weight issue can often be a focus for or distraction from feelings connected with other areas of our life.

Equally, carrying extra fat can place a layer of protective padding between ourselves and the rest of the world. This hides and disguises feelings of vulnerability, acting as a barrier to uncomfortable events and feelings. Not surprisingly, the times in our lives when we weigh the most often relate to periods of emotional difficulty. Being overweight can also represent surplus 'baggage'. The unresolved or unexpressed emotions that we store in our bodies are like a build-up of excess material that we have yet to assimilate.

Whichever way you look at it, emotional and psychological issues have a direct link to the success of a weight loss programme. Since there are many different aspects to weight loss, a multi-faceted approach is called for. You can use EFT for:

- Motivation and Resistance
- Cravings
- Self-belief
- Sabotage
- Underlying Causes

## PAST
### MEMORIES

Too many diets and weight loss programmes can feel like forms of punishment. Deprivation and starvation are not likely to be attractive or succeed as long-term solutions to a weight problem. Starving the body does not effectively sustain weight loss – in fact it causes the opposite. The body is more likely to hold on to its reserves if food intake is reduced.

The good news is that with EFT, achieving weight loss is never about willpower. If you address the areas that prevent success, weight loss should occur easily, consistently and with minimal distress. Eating a sensible and healthy diet should become a natural and desired outcome.

One of the first concepts to understand is that a body that is rejected and criticized by you is not a body that will co-operate with your desires. If you are always belittling the way you look, your body will become your enemy. A loving and supportive communication needs to take place to promote a more healthy relationship.

Our thoughts shape our reality so if you believe you are fat, then that will be your reality. If you tell your body how fat you are every time you look in the mirror, that is what will be reflected back to you. Changing your attitude will change your reality. Encourage yourself to head in the direction you want to go, rather than insulting yourself for where you are now.

In order to lose weight you need to discover what being overweight means to you and what attitudes are contributing to it. If you release the psychology that keeps the weight in place, you will start to see changes in your physical shape. Below are some questions and suggestions to look at. They will not all apply to you, but they will help you to reflect on areas in which you could use EFT.

- When did you start to gain weight?
- What was going on in your life around this time?
- Were there any feelings you were attempting to hide from, avoid or stuff down?
- What does the weight protect you from?
- What is the weight hiding?
- If there was an aspect of you that the weight disguised what would that be?

## WHAT DO YOU BELIEVE?

Negative beliefs can prevent weight loss. This is because unconstructive beliefs cause our energy circuits to reverse. The knock-on effect of this is that we do the opposite of what we are hoping to achieve. So, instead of losing weight, we remain the same size or, in the worst cases, gain even more weight.

Have a look at the following statements and rate how true each one is for you out of ten. This will illustrate how strongly your beliefs are holding you back.

'I don't believe I can lose weight.'
'I don't believe I can be a success.'
'I have a physical reason for my weight problem.'
'I don't lose weight easily.'
'I have a slow metabolism.'
'It's my age.'
'I gain weight easily.'
'I don't believe I can get my figure back.'

Now, take a few moments to write down any personal beliefs you have about weight loss. To help, you could ask:

- How do you view being slender?
- What does being slim imply to you?
- What do you think about other people who are slim?
- How would you feel if you were slim?
- If all the weight you are hoping to lose was magically lifted away what feelings would it take with it?

Once you have a list, grade your level of belief in each item out of ten. The higher the score, the more interference that particular belief will have regarding your results. Are there any other areas of your life in which you feel the same way? Do you perceive any connection? Did you discover any thoughts or feelings that were not positive? If you did, use your findings to identify the issues that can be cleared with EFT. Turn each of the negative thoughts into a Set-up statement and use the tapping technique to remove the beliefs that are holding you back.

## Motivation and Resistance

An area that often stops us achieving our ideal size is motivation. Many people find that the lack of motivation to begin a weight loss regime is the very thing preventing them from starting. There are a hundred and one reasons not to. What excuses are your favourites?

'I don't have the will power.'
'I don't have the time.'

'I don't have the money to join a gym.'
'I'm too tired.'
'I can't be bothered.'
'It's too expensive to buy separate food for myself.'
'I love junk food.'
'I enjoy alcohol.'
'I hate exercise.'
'I don't like healthy foods.'
'It is too much hassle to prepare separate meals.'
'I prepare foods that please my partner.'

Identify all the reasons why you resist starting a weight-loss programme. List all the ways you sabotage yourself. Then give each one a score out of ten to grade the intensity or level of belief you have in each one. Place *'Even though …'* in front of them and you will have an emotionally charged statement to work on. Clearing your resistance will mean that you feel more enthusiastic about taking the first step.

## Cravings

Whether your Achilles heel is chocolate, cream cakes, wine or cheese, EFT is a good way to reduce cravings that sabotage your best intentions. A common result of using this technique is a balancing of appetite. One of our clients was impressed with the fact that she could now leave food on her plate when she felt full. Before, she had always felt the need to finish every last mouthful. She connected this behaviour with being told as a child that you should 'never waste food'. The belief had stuck at an unconscious level, making her feel uncomfortable if she left any food.

emotional healing

### lucy's story – compulsive eating

A case of compulsive eating disorder was presented by John Burik on the EFT website. It involved Lucy, a middle-aged lady who had tried many different diets, lasting from four months duration to over a year. Her average weight loss over this period was an average of half a pound a week. She agreed to take part in a trial for nine weeks and this involved tapping four times a day, as well as the times when she experienced urges to compulsively eat. As a result she lost seven and a half pounds over the nine-week period. This was an improvement on her previous diet attempts. She also remarked that since beginning the EFT there had been absolutely no incidents of compulsive eating.

Routinely tapping throughout the day does seem to produce a marked improvement. Here are some statements that you may find useful:

'Even though food is my way of coping/distracting myself I deeply and completely accept myself.'
'Even though I crave chocolate/sweets/cakes/wine I deeply and completely accept myself.'
'Even though I snack I deeply and completely accept myself.'
'Even though I get hungry late at night I deeply and completely accept myself.'
'Even though I never feel full I deeply and completely accept myself.'

### Reducing Cravings

Cravings can be addressed as part of a treatment plan throughout the day or as you experience them.

To reduce a craving the first thing you need to do is rate your desire for the substance out of ten. This gives you a guideline to work from. Ask yourself what you crave about the item. Place the substance in front of you, smell it, taste a little of it, look at it continuously, while using the basic tapping technique for:

'Even though I want this ... I deeply and completely accept myself.'

Afterwards, carry out an entire round for the remaining craving until it fades:

'Even though I still really want this ... I deeply and completely accept myself.'

The desire for the article should diminish with each tapping round. Simply tapping the Gamut point while focusing on the craving or item can be sufficient, but it is advisable to do a complete round of EFT when in the initial stages of eradicating a strong craving. Use this approach to work through the foods that you can't seem to resist. Apply EFT regularly throughout the day, as well as at the specific times when you need extra support. Tailor the technique to the areas you need help with to produce your own personal programme.

## Self-belief

A common area that may also produce an obstacle to attaining your ideal figure is self-belief. We all have negative thoughts from time to time, but too much negativity can create Psychological Reversal, preventing us from achieving the very thing we most desire. Catching our negative self-talk can be quite difficult, as thoughts come and go so quickly. Here are some common ones that you might recognize:

'I don't deserve to be my ideal weight.'
'I will always be overweight.'
'People of my age lose their figure.'
'I never keep these things going.'
'I always end up the same.'
'I haven't got the perseverance.'
'I've got no self-control.'
'Things never work for me.'
'No matter how hard I try, I never lose weight.'

Some of these may *seem* true to you, but they are just beliefs holding you back. If you are going to listen to beliefs then let them be positive ones, such as *'I lose weight easily'*. How much do you believe that statement out of ten? Dissolve every thought, belief or attitude that prevents you from believing ten out of ten that *'I lose weight easily'* with the standard EFT routine.

### Mirror, Mirror …

A good way to elicit an emotional charge is to look at yourself in a mirror. Take a good look at yourself. What do you say to yourself about your body?

'I hate my thighs/hips/bottom.'
'I'm fat.'
'I'm ugly/grotesque/revolting.'

Clearing this negative self-talk will make you feel better, as well as removing the energetic disturbance that this kind of thinking creates. It can be a very powerful exercise to stand naked in front of the mirror while using EFT.

## Sabotage

As hard as it is to believe, at some level being overweight can be a choice. As with Psychological Reversal, it may not be an intended choice, but it is a choice nonetheless. Not being slim may allow us to continue unhealthy behaviours or it can be a way of hiding or avoiding being noticed. The weight may be a result of comforting ourselves with food or as a consequence of denying ourselves physical exercise. Being large can prevent others from getting too close, physically as well as emotionally. Regardless of how unhappy being overweight makes you, there are still pay-offs to the condition. These secondary gains contribute to Psychological Reversal and are likely to be confusing to the energy system. What are your pay-offs?

'I get to eat what I want, when I want.'
'I don't have to exercise.'
'Men don't give me too much sexual attention.'
'I get to feel sorry for myself.'
'I don't have to make an effort.'
'I get to make excuses.'

Any pay-off will need to be resolved in order to be successful. After applying EFT to the most obvious hidden gains, you could try muscle testing or taking a truth test for general statements such as:

'It is now safe for me to lose weight.'
'I now release all blocks to losing weight.'
'I want to lose weight.'
'I am prepared to do what ever it takes to lose weight.'

emotional healing

Self-sabotage is very common in any form of dietary or exercise regime. It is very easy to become de-motivated and unenthusiastic. As you become skilful in the art of applying EFT, you will discover that there is no negative emotion that EFT cannot be used to balance. If you are sabotaging your own progress, start tapping!

## Underlying Causes of Overweight

If you have to stay on a diet in order to be slim, you are not getting to the root of the problem. You are only suppressing or palliating it. Look for the underlying reason – it could be emotional, motivational, dietary or a combination of factors. In a cause-and-effect universe there is a reason for everything. There is a possibility that you have certain physical or energetic allergies that are causing you to gain weight. There could be a fundamental emotional reason or it could simply be that you are not using up sufficient energy to maintain a trim figure. Either way, if you have a weight problem, there will be a cause that you can work on with EFT. So you need to discover the appropriate area to focus on.

## MAPPING YOUR WEIGHT HISTORY

Create your own weight map. Look back over your history to discover how your size reflects life events. Are you happiest when you're thinner or larger? Were there any other times in your life when you put on weight and, if so, is there any similarity to your life now? How do stress, relationship difficulties and work problems affect you?

There may also be memories of failed weight-loss attempts that come back to plague you when you think of changing your lifestyle. A favourite statement used by one of our friends was *'I only ever lose a few pounds, I can never shift the weight on my thighs.'* We asked her how strongly she believed these statements and were told they were both ten out of ten statements – in other words, 'absolute truths'. If this is the area you are having difficulty with, rebalance your outlook to the current situation by resolving the feelings of failure. Some useful statements may be:

'Even though I keep remembering how I failed before I deeply and completely accept myself.'
'Even though I only lost two pounds last time I deeply and completely accept myself.'
'Even though I don't see the point of trying again I deeply and completely accept myself.'

Just as illness can be an indication that all is not well, excess weight can also be a sign that something in our lives needs more attention. EFT will do a great deal to ensure that food, cravings and emotional issues stop ruining your attempts to be the size and shape you want to be. It will also neutralize the unconscious sabotage that creates the opposite of what you are trying to achieve. By adjusting your energy system, you can turn a frustrated and unhealthy obsession with weight loss into appropriate action that is pleasurable and life enhancing.

## Chapter 14

# Relationships

Our relationships have a direct influence on our emotional happiness and well-being. From our partners, through to parents and work colleagues, the quality of our relationships is probably the most important feature in our lives. Nowhere are emotions so intricately involved than with our personal relationships with others. When a relationship goes wrong or becomes strained, our emotions are usually thrown into turmoil.

## FAMILY FEUDS

Sometimes irreparable damage is caused by something that just slipped out of our mouths before we could stop it and we wish we could take it all back or turn back the clock. Arguments can lead to people refusing to talk to family; former friends, lovers and work colleagues, because of upsets and hurts that seem 'unforgivable'. Sometimes people even take their anger and hurt to the grave with them. Many families have been divided by harsh words or cruel comments that have caused a weeping wound, which becomes difficult to heal. Unfortunately, you can't change what has happened in the past, but you can change the way you feel about it.

Such rifts can start with an angry or disrespectful word, spoken at a time when we are tired or stressed, or because we are concerned with a situation which is not under our control. Someone says the wrong thing and because we are 'irritated' (our energy system is disturbed by our worried thoughts) an argument may start and reach a peak when the most harmful words are used.

When the argument is over, the emotionally wounded parties separate. The argument is then replayed over and over in our minds, *'How could he/she have said this'* and *'I wish I had said that'*, further compounding our emotions. Each time we think about that person, the memory of what happened causes a disruption in our energy system and we feel as bad as we did when the original argument occurred. The next time we meet we may try to put it all behind us, but through gritted teeth (using will-power), the atmosphere is strained and conversations stilted. A disagreeable look or comment may be all that is needed to start the row again, causing the rift to widen.

Once the core issues of an embittered relationship have been resolved with the help of EFT, and all the resentment has been tapped away, there is nothing left to fuel the fire. The true cause of disputes usually derives from basic emotions such as hurt, anger, betrayal or feeling unloved. These fundamental issues are at the root of most disagreements but it is only after removing the surface emotions that this becomes apparent.

With the help of EFT, it is easy to lay past grievances to rest, bringing genuine peace to even the most volatile relationships or embittered grievances. It can take only a few minutes to tap away the emotions that could potentially cause so much damage.

Of course, it is much better if relationships never get to this crisis point. If we pay attention to how we are feeling and take notice of the things that perturb us before they get out of proportion, we can prevent hurting ourselves as well as those we love. Tapping for feelings as they first surface will give you vital insight into the true cause of the problem. If this all sounds too simple, it's because it is, but we often leave the most important things to last.

## Stress Barometer

A good way of monitoring your emotions is to design your own barometer in your mind. You can instruct this barometer to alert you whenever negative emotions are starting to effect you. If the zero to ten scale is used you can set the barometer at a certain level to alert you to distress. For example, let's say four out of ten is when you usually start to become tense. The next time something begins to upset you, a psychological alarm can go off, reminding you that you have reached four out of ten on your distress level. Start tapping the emotional pressure away immediately until you are back to a zero. This can help to prevent stress and uncomfortable emotions boiling over unnecessarily and remove the need for conflict with those closest to you.

# PAST
# RELATIONSHIPS

Relationships can be an emotional minefield. Failed relationships can leave psychological scars which take many years to heal. When a relationship breaks down, numerous emotions can be experienced:

| | |
|---|---|
| abandonment | hurt |
| anger | loss |
| betrayal | regret |
| despair | resentment |
| disappointment | self-blame |
| grief | shock |
| humiliation | unrequited love |

A broken heart can feel devastating – as if the end of the world has come – especially if you have invested vast amounts of time and energy into the relationship. If children are involved this can bring additional heartache. At times like these, friends can unwittingly take sides leaving you with very little in the way of support. Suddenly, there is no longer an 'us', but only an 'I', and you can feel totally lost.

Almost every level of existence then undergoes a radical adjustment as you learn to live on your own again. This can cause immense suffering and loneliness. In this situation, using EFT on a daily basis can help you to come to terms with the end of a relationship. It is also beneficial to use the technique to resolve anything that has been left unsaid or to 'mop up' an overspill of emotions. Dissipating these overwhelming emotions can help you recover emotionally unscathed and start moving forward towards a positive future.

Jonathan experienced his first taste of heartbreak in his late teens. If left unresolved, these early relationships splits can leave an extremely vivid emotional memory late into adulthood.

### jonathan's story – broken heart
'Not long ago, I was going through a rough patch. It was caused by a dead-end job and the lack of a girlfriend. Then I was introduced to Kim …

'As she walked into the room, it was as if time stood still. I experienced a moment of clarity. As I looked into her eyes the words formed in my mouth "Will you go out with me?" It seemed like an eternity for her to answer. Eventually, she said "Yes".

'For the first few months of our relationship, things were great and I was really happy. Then one day she looked very worried, so I asked her what was wrong. She told me that she was pregnant by her previous boyfriend. I remember the relief on her face when I said, "I'm not going anywhere, I'll stand by you." Two weeks later she told me that she had miscarried. Once again I reassured her that I was here and that I still loved her.

'A few days after this, she came into my workplace and told me we were finished. It felt like my whole world was walking away as she turned to leave. I felt so angry and all manner of different emotions – loneliness, rejection, used, and completely unwanted. I felt totally on the edge and cursed God for letting this happen. I had never felt so low. I honestly wanted to die. I didn't care anymore and just wanted a way out. I was taken to the doctor but the antidepressants he prescribed had no effect. So I started taking recreational drugs. I became a recluse, not wanting to leave my house. I tried counselling but that didn't help either. The only thing that killed the pain was getting so "high" that I didn't know where I was.

'Then a friend suggested EFT. I had never heard of it before but was willing to try anything to get myself back together. During the session I relayed the entire account. Paul instructed me to tap every time I experienced any distressing emotions.

I tapped for *"Even though Kim left me I deeply and completely accept myself."* This statement really helped me. I felt as though a great weight had been lifted from my shoulders. The feelings of pain subsided and I could think clearly again. From this viewpoint I was able to see the whole situation as a learning experience.

'I suddenly felt a warmth inside that I feared had long perished. When I left, instead of going home I went off into town – I had left my reclusive ways behind! In just one session I now had the confidence to step back into the world again. Although I still had some feelings left for Kim, I hardly noticed them. Since the treatment I have made peace with God and myself. I am also back in control of my life.'

We all desire to be loved, to love another and share our lives with someone. However, being in love and sharing can leave us feeling vulnerable and this can strike fear in to the bravest of us. Many people find it hard to express or show love at the best of times. So when we have been hurt we question whether we can ever trust someone again. If this happens repeatedly we can put up barriers to keep love out, but we end up feeling cut off and lonely.

Learning to re-open your heart is vital. If we don't heal our past there is the possibility we will contaminate our next relationship with our unresolved feelings. Our emotional hang-ups become like old friends that are difficult to leave behind. A large proportion of relationship problems have nothing to do with the current two people involved, but are the result of residual conflicts from previous failed relationships.

# THE PAIR
# OF YOU

Like attracts like, so the significant others in our lives represent a reflection of certain aspects of ourselves. This is because relationships are ultimately intended to have a healing nature. Amongst other things, our partner mirrors back to us the things we most dislike about ourselves. This may be the hardest thing to recognize and admit because we intentionally suppress these unwanted traits. When you come together you are both confronted with the parts of your personalities that need to be healed. As a result you become irritated with all your partner's negative traits and they will highlight all the things they dislike about you.

Even though you both share similar issues, you will not necessarily recognize the fact. You may not show your 'selfishness' in the same way as your partner or not be 'judgmental' about the same things, but there will still be a resonance of some kind. Each of you will possess the undesired trait but express it in a different way. The things you accuse your partner of are the flaws within yourself that you are most likely to deny. So it would be wise to heed the saying 'When you point a finger in blame, three point back at you.'

## Relationship Conflict

When a relationship deteriorates it can be very easy to point the finger of blame at our partner. Often we delude ourselves that if only *they* would change, our lives would be fine; if only they were a better listener, a better lover or do more around the house, the relationship would improve. As long as we believe it's all *their* fault, we avoid looking to ourselves for the answer. And it is impossible to change anyone other than oneself.

If you and your partner are discussing a problem and one of you begins to get angry, things can suddenly spiral out of control. Before you know it, it has erupted into a row. Once an argument begins, neither of you will truly listen to the other. Usually one person will become angry while the other feels hurt. The angry party brings out ammunition from all of those stored-up hurts they've been holding on to, kept for times such as this. As a result the other person feels under attack and becomes even more defensive. It ends up with one of you saying 'I give in' or both of you storming off in a huff and not speaking to each other. Nobody wins, both of you end up feeling resentful and nothing gets resolved.

## Breaking the Vicious Circle

For things to change, one of you needs to take responsibility for not letting the situation get out of hand. It's not about control or someone winning but about breaking the cycle. This might not be easy at first, but if you both want the relationship to work it is worth the effort. It takes the energy of two people to have an argument but only one of you needs to say *'Stop!'* If both parties spent five minutes tapping away their indignation, self-righteousness or feelings of hurt, the situation would calm down considerably. Even if just one of you taps for how you are feeling it will be enough to defuse the energy. Clearing the energetic charge will remove or take the edge off inflamed emotions and allow you to view the situation from a different per-spective. Once the emotional reactions are diffused, you can start talking to each other again – only this time you will be surprised how much calmer you both are.

Frequently we expect our partner to fulfil needs within us that are the result of other people's misconduct. When our partner inevitably fails to do this we can feel angry and resentful that they haven't lived up to our expectations. May was in her late sixties and was now in her second marriage. She was very unhappy and often complained and moaned about what her husband was 'doing' or 'not doing right'. Because of her age and the fact that she had felt miserable almost all her life she didn't feel that tapping certain places on her body would help her.

### may's story – old resentments

'For as long as I can remember I have felt unhappy, angry, bitter and resentful. I attended one of Val's self-awareness groups and listened to the other members talking about EFT. It had helped them to improve their relationships as well as their emotional problems. Even though I could see others moving through their emotions, I refused Val's offer of help. One reason for this was that I didn't like change – it scared me – and besides, I couldn't see why it was me that had to change! It wasn't my fault. I believed that if my husband changed, my life would be much better. I blamed him for my unhappiness and everyone else for all the things that had gone wrong in my life.

'As time went by I became worse. I was more irritable than ever before and would cry for no reason. Eventually I put my hand up and asked for help. During the session I was shocked to realize how much I had blamed my husband for my present unhappiness. It was so much easier to pick holes in him than actually tackle my real problem. I recognized that it was the relationship with myself that needed addressing. No matter what he did, it would never be enough to make me feel better. As the emotions cleared, I suddenly felt sorry that I had made both of us so miserable. It didn't have to be this way. Even though I believed I was too old to change or be happy,

I tapped for the ingrained beliefs that were keeping me from finding the happiness I so desperately wanted.

'To my surprise, I did gradually start to change. I know I have a lifetime of suppressed emotions to resolve and I am prepared for this. For now, I am much less angry and stressed. When I become irritated I use the tapping technique instead of sulking or feeling sorry for myself. I have stopped criticizing my husband so much and I'm sure he has noticed the positive changes in me. I have taken responsibility for my own sadness and our relationship is improving because of it. I've also come to understand that you can't blame anyone else for the feelings inside you. I now like and believe in myself much more. I feel happier inside and, most importantly, I am now prepared to look at my true self and tap for anything that distresses me. Thank you EFT. I am not too old after all.'

**Talking Stick**

A Native American practice that is beneficial when communicating with each other is to use a 'Talking Stick'. This is a stick of wood that is used to indicate who has the right to speak. When a person is holding the talking stick, everyone else must actively listen without interruption. Once the person feels they have had ample time to put their point across, they then hand the stick to the next person whose turn it is to speak.

In discussing relationship problems, passing the stick back and forth in this way enables both parties to air their views without the fear of accusation or interruption. It also ensures that when your partner is talking, your attention is focused on what they are trying to say rather than planning your next retort. It is not important that you use a stick – anything will do. Using an object in this way creates healthy boundaries and the vital space each of you need to express your individual feelings.

Working on your relationship will take time and patience. Learning to recognize when to tap rather than continue with a disagreement is a skill but it is one worth learning. The outcome will be a happy and fulfilling relationship on every level.

## Working as a Couple

A very powerful approach to repairing a relationship is to use the technique in unison with your partner. This involves facing your partner while you both tap on each others' meridian points. This can be a moving emotional experience for both partners, especially when working on mutual concerns such as financial difficulties or problems with children. Decide what issue you would both like to work on and simultaneously tap on each other. Whether we realize it or not, a lot of our emotional concerns are issues that we share. For instance, you may believe that it is your partner who has an issue of jealousy, even though you fail to recognize the same issue in yourself. This is probably because you don't acknowledge or convey your jealousy in the same way. The fact that you are together means that there are a lot of similarities between you, but your emotions may come across in different ways. Tapping together can clear a problem for the pair of you on both conscious and unconscious levels. Once all the negative emotions are resolved you may realize that the silly things you previously argued about are irrelevant. All that really matters is the love between you.

## Annoying Habits

We can all be irritated by something our partner does. It is a natural part of living together. However these minor annoyances needn't build up out of proportion or become bigger issues than they really are. Removing the emotional disruption that results from 'infuriating' habits can help you to reduce the level of frustration and handle the situation appropriately without losing your composure. Here are some examples to illustrate how you can create an emotionally charged statement for each situation. Notice that when applying EFT for your reaction to someone else's behaviour, '*I deeply and completely accept him/her*' can be used. This promotes acceptance of the person – even with their irritating behaviour.

> 'Even though Richard always leaves the toilet seat up I deeply and completely accept him.'
> 'Even though Tina's bedroom is a complete mess I deeply and completely accept her.'
> 'Even though Sue is always nagging me to tidy up I deeply and completely accept her.'
> 'Even though I feel so irritated with Henry I deeply and completely accept him.'

The list is endless. Try it for yourself. You can't change others but you can prevent yourself from becoming unnecessarily frustrated. Taking the emotional charge away from the situation will enable the pair of you to live together much more harmoniously. It will also help to heal unresolved emotions from the past and remove dysfunctional reactions and unhealthy behaviour patterns.

The arena of relationships can be an emotional battlefield at times. Unconstructive emotions can stand in the way of growing together and can prevent you from adapting and truly listening to your partner's and your own needs. EFT can act as an antidote to these stressful emotions, allowing you to take down your barriers and see your relationship problems from a balanced perspective.

**Chapter 15**

# Troubleshooting

This chapter has been designed to assist you when a physical or emotional complaint is failing to respond to the treatment straight away. As long as your score of emotional intensity is dropping, the technique is working. If at any stage the level of discomfort remains the same or if no improvement is gained, there is an evident block interfering with the procedure. There are several factors that can hinder progress.

## CHOOSING YOUR STATEMENT

The first obstacle may be the statement that you are using.

### Be Specific with Your Statements

The opening statement you choose must be as specific as possible. Sometimes people are too general with their statements. When constructing a statement you need to include specific characteristics of your physical or emotional issue, rather than using a term that refers to the whole thing. For example,

'Even though I have Irritable Bowel Syndrome ...'

may produce fairly discouraging results and not be sufficient to address your current abdominal discomfort. An affirmation stating,

'Even though I have burning stomach cramps I deeply and completely accept myself.'

is much more likely to produce relief.

Being specific enables you to focus on one particular issue at a time and clear it accordingly. This is much easier than trying to resolve the entire problem in one concerted effort. Muscle cramps, irritability, sadness and apprehension all produce different energetic patterns and disruptions within the meridian system. Addressing a problem that contains all these characteristics at once would be very confusing. Specific statements allow you to clear each unique energy disturbance individually in a methodical way.

## Addressing Your Situation, Not Your Intention

To achieve the best results, your statement needs to produce a disruption within the energy system. This is why stating your positive intent does not work as well as stating the negative current emotion. *I want to feel peaceful* is a nice desire to aim for, but repeating this phrase will not produce a disruption within the body. Choose a sentence that describes your present feelings, thoughts and sensations explicitly. Be as honest as you can with yourself, even if you are embarrassed to admit how you feel. The more accurate the statement, the more significant the change will be.

Using your own words will also enhance the affirmation process. These are the words you use on a regular basis to express how you feel; they may make little sense to anyone else, but should have vital significance for you. If you tend to describe your internal condition as '*wobbly*', the most productive statement would include '*this wobbly feeling*'. Or, if you often complain of a '*dodgy stomach*', adding the word '*dodgy*' to the affirmation will make it more potent. This can be particularly relevant if English is not your first language. As was the case with Heidi, who was born in Germany.

### heidi's story – language barrier

Heidi had booked a session with us to clear some emotional problems. The session was progressing nicely until Heidi had a revelation about being German:

'I have lived in the UK for 14 years and people compliment me on my nearly accent-free English. I never thought this was particularly significant until I realized I did not feel proud of my German heritage and that I had spent much of the last 14 years denying it. I had no German friends in England and 'failed' to bring up my daughter bilingually. I felt that as a German I was much hated and ridiculed in this country. In fact, I felt I had to hide the fact that I was German. After being exposed to the same jokes and taunts for 14 years, I realized that I had made myself as un-German as possible. Hence the fact that I spoke perfect English and my daughter hardly spoke any German at all.'

During the session Heidi's emotional intensity stopped reducing after several tapping rounds. Heidi realized that the incident she was recalling happened while she was very young and still living in Germany, so the statements needed to be spoken in German. This had more impact and progress was achieved once more.

'After my EFT session I truly accepted the fact that I was German. I could even see the funny side to all this. Consequently, I also made several friendships with some German people who also lived in the UK.'

## Emphasis

The way you say the statement may also influence the results. Make sure that you repeat the statement out loud every time you change the tapping location. Repeating the statement half-heartedly or in an indifferent manner may prevent it from working. Even if you don't believe what you are saying or find it difficult state the affirmation, it is vital that you repeat the phrase with *enthusiasm and conviction*. Putting some energy into your statement is very important.

Find the part of you that really wants to change and tap into its resources. The more intent you are on resolving your problem, the quicker the emotional intensity will drop. We have found that, when necessary, shouting the statement can break the stalemate and produce an energetic shift.

# HIDDEN ASPECTS

Quite often people conclude that EFT has failed to work, when, in fact, additional facets to the problem have arisen that need to be treated as individual aspects.

Some EFT sessions are comparatively simple. As you tap for the presenting problem, you may only need to address a few different aspects to remove the issue entirely. However, some issues are more complicated because of the number of contributing aspects. Identifying all of them may require persistence and a detective-like curiosity. Complete relief is not always obtained until all the different aspects that feed the problem are collapsed. Check that there are no hidden aspects to the issue that are holding it in place.

Sometimes, the conflict you have tapped for is no longer the issue you are experiencing. It is likely that you have switched to another aspect or layer of the problem without your knowing. You need to take a methodical approach, clearing each layer individually, removing every aspect that contributes to the overall difficulty. As long as the aspects you are working on are diminishing in emotional intensity, you are moving in the right direction. If they are changing focus you are definitely eliminating the original problem. However, if you are unsure whether this applies to you, go back over the aspects that you have previously tapped for to see if they are still an issue for you. It may also be helpful to review the problem with a friend. Talking it through can reveal hidden or related aspects that you may have missed the first time.

# PSYCHOLOGICAL REVERSAL

Psychological Reversal could also be interfering with your results. It is essential for the Set-Up to be performed correctly at the beginning of each tapping round. If the Set-Up is not applied correctly, the rest of the procedure may be ineffective. The Set-Up primes the meridian system for adjustments to be made. It also aligns your conscious desire with your unconscious intentions.

If you suspect that Psychological Reversal is preventing you from overcoming your difficulty, perform some additional round adjustments for the Psychological Reversal before actually addressing the problem. Also re-read the chapter on Psychological Reversal (Chapter 7).

In cases where there is considerable Psychological Reversal connected with a particular issue (too many secondary gains), try EFT for another subject first. This will serve to build your confidence in the process. Once you are obtaining relief from other problems, the meridian system is more open and receptive to change. Spontaneously swapping to the problem that is resisting treatment takes the issue 'by surprise' and allows it to be cleared before the energy flow has had time to reverse.

## Modifications

Modifying the Set-up may also be useful; try swapping to the alternative Set-Up procedure. If you have been using the Karate Chop point while repeating your affirmation, change to the Tender Spot (or vice versa) to see if this makes a difference.

Within our practice we have modified the Gamut procedure to suit our needs. However, there are some occasions where using Gary Craig's comprehensive Gamut formula can be beneficial. If a problem is very difficult to shift, there are a couple of techniques that will make it more effective. This involves the addition of humming and counting to five, at certain stages, while tapping the Gamut point. Although this may appear quite strange at first, these two procedures have a balancing effect on the brain. Just as moving the eyes in different directions stimulates certain parts of the brain, when you hum the right side of the brain is engaged, and when you count the left side of the brain is activated. Incorporating both sides of the brain can enhance the clearing effects and remove stubborn psychological blocks. Here is Gary Craig's original Gamut procedure.

# THE COMPREHENSIVE GAMUT PROCEDURE

After performing the usual Set-Up and Sequence of tapping, simultaneously tap the Gamut point while performing the following steps:

**1** Close your eyes.

**2** Open your eyes.

**3** While holding your head still look hard down right.

**4** While holding your head still look hard down left.

**5** Keeping your head perfectly still, roll your eyes anti-clockwise in a complete circle.

**6** Repeat again, rolling your eyes in a complete circle in a clockwise direction.

**7** For a few seconds, hum your favourite song or hum the words to 'Happy Birthday'.

**8** Count rapidly from one to five.

**9** Hum aloud for another few seconds.

If you find the complete Gamut technique more successful, it can be used to replace the shortened version.

# CORE
## ISSUES

The art of EFT is tapping for the right issues. One factor that can prevent total resolution from a difficulty is an underlying core issue. There are times when a fundamental problem is concealed by a less important presenting complaint. As long as a core issue exists, the presenting problem will remain intact. You may start tapping for a presenting complaint, only to find that each emotional memory leads you further back towards the root cause. All sorts of memories may then start queuing up to be cleared. This is an excellent opportunity for you to understand clearly why you have the resulting problem. James' Public Speaking phobia is a case in point.

### james' story – public speaking phobia

James, a 35-year-old civil servant, describes himself as extremely shy. He would blush, sweat, shake and stutter whenever he was in a group situation. These feelings would intensify if the group turned their attention on him or if he was required to speak. When in this situation his throat would begin to close up and he would feel extremely uncomfortable. An opportunity arose that would improve his income, but it required teaching small groups of people. James knew that this would be virtually impossible for him if he did not attempt to overcome his fear of public speaking. He decided to try EFT and set about breaking his fear into different aspects:

- The fear of forgetting his words.
- The fear of what others were thinking about him.
- The fear that the audience would be bored.
- The closing up feeling in his throat.

- The butterflies in his stomach.
- The terrifying thought of doing a talk.

He then applied a complete EFT round to each aspect. He discovered that his feelings about the upcoming engagement were greatly improved and he was able to go ahead with the small teaching groups.

Although he felt a lot better, he still had to use will-power to overcome the nervousness that was still present. He searched for hidden aspects to the fear that he might have missed in the previous tapping sessions, but he could only come up with a vague feeling of fear that he couldn't pin down to one particular issue. He explained the feeling as a faceless fear that defied description. He was confident enough to continue with his teaching events, but felt that somewhere along the line a vital issue had not been addressed. On reflection, James noticed that there was a certain picture that repeatedly flashed into his mind. It was a memory of performing on stage when he was eight. He was dressed in a Native American costume and was made to dance around in front of his classmates. James cringed at the mere thought of this. As soon as he realized that this was important, he began tapping for all the aspects of the uncomfortable memory. He applied an individual round for:

- The traumatic stage memory.
- The blind panic.
- Feeling undignified.
- The fact that he was made to do it.
- The fact that he had to wear make up in front of everybody.
- People were laughing at him.

After a few minutes of tapping, the emotional charge connected with this distressing event had completely cleared. As
a result, his fear of public speaking was entirely resolved. He
was then able to increase his teaching hours and perform
without the usual nerves. Speaking in front of groups ceased
to be a problem for him.

We often describe the core issue of a problem as the 'queen bee' that all
the other fears serve. One characteristic that signifies the presence of a core
issue is the vague sensation that a problem is not resolved. A good technique to use here is to ask yourself more questions around the subject in
question.

- What lies underneath all these other emotions?
- What is the most fundamental problem?
- What do you see happening to yourself?
- Does this present problem remind you of any
  other time in your life?
- How does this current situation remind you of ____
  another time?
- If you had to guess what was preventing you
  from overcoming this problem what would it be?

If a problem remains the same after the umpteenth time of tapping, ask
yourself what memory, if healed, would enable you to walk away free of the
problem once and for all? Then let the thought go – think about something
else. When you are least expecting it, you may get an unconscious answer
to your question. Trust in your unconscious mind. Once you have connected with a memory that seems important, tap for it, even if it seems absurd,
and tap for the feelings that it evokes. Pay attention to these flashbacks,
they are important. Tap for all the feelings connected to a flashback memory

and see where it leads you. Be aware of any memories or associations that come to light. Apply the technique to the root cause and the surface problem should resolve.

# ENERGY
## TOXINS

For a small minority (about five per cent of the population) EFT can be rendered ineffective because a toxic substance of some kind is distorting the energy system. An individual can be susceptible to almost any known substance from french fries to bananas. It is not necessarily the common culprits that we normally see as 'bad' or 'unhealthy'. It is just as likely to be peppers, tomatoes or oranges. Ingesting or coming in contact with the substance can cause a form of energetic allergic reaction. This allergic response is not usually strong enough to produce physical symptoms, but is potent enough to interfere on an energetic level. Having said that, some conditions including depression, sleep disorders and panic attacks can be traced directly to energy toxins. Once eliminated from their lives, people have found their symptoms cease within a few days. We all have different sensitivities – some people are affected by toxins in the environment, while others have reactions to certain foods. The most frequently found energy toxins include:

| | |
|---|---|
| additives and preservatives | deodorant |
| aerosol emissions | diary |
| alcohol | electronic devices |
| chemicals | medications |
| coffee | microwave ovens |
| computers | mobile phones |
| cosmetics | perfume |

emotional healing

pesticides  
recreational drugs  
soap  
solvents  
sugar  

synthetic fibres  
tea  
televisions  
wheat  

A strong indication of an energy toxin blocking progress is an issue consistently returning after you have tapped it away. You may have gained partial or total relief from a problem only to have it come back a while later. This is not the usual way that EFT works. Once an issue is completely resolved it stays that way. When energy toxins are involved the *complete problem* returns, not just a new aspect. Also, if EFT appears to work one day but not the next, it is probably because there is toxic interference within the meridian system. If you suspect that energy toxins are upsetting your progress there are several approaches that you can employ:

- Move from where you are currently sitting in case electronic or environmental influences are present.
- Drink a glass of water. This can help to flush out the system.
- Apply EFT when you are wearing no cosmetics, hairspray, perfume or deodorant.
- Before re-applying the technique take a bath, shower or remove your clothing.
- Wait a day or two and try again. In the meantime eat and drink in moderation.

Sometimes you may already have an idea of what substance is detrimental to you. It could be the thing you crave or something you use on a daily basis. If you think that dietary factors may be to blame, visit a qualified kinesiologist who can discover the exact products that should be avoided. Eliminating the culprit from your diet or environment for a minimum of three days should be sufficient to regain energetic balance and therefore benefit from EFT. It will then be vital to monitor your progress before re-introducing the toxin into your system in case it brings the old symptoms back.

# NEUROLOGICAL DISORGANIZATION

In a very small number of cases, a condition known as Neurological Disorganization prevents EFT from working. Neurological Disorganization is the term used to describe a type of overload or short circuit within the system. Brain signals and energy patterns become confused, creating a form of electrical storm in which the energy flow is jumbled and non-directional. You may have experienced a similar sensation if suddenly asked for directions. Working out which way is left and which is right can take a moment to work out. Similarly, when under stress the ability to think clearly, spell or respond to questions can be very difficult. We experience Neurological Disorganization as feelings of disorientation, indecision and confusion. Often this condition will arise when dealing with intense emotional issues. Every time you try to think about your problem, you feel overwhelmed, confused and unable to think straight. This indicates emotional overload.

When Neurological Disorganization is present the energy flow through the meridians is completely scrambled. This makes EFT balancing impossible. In the same way as the reversed energy flow of Psychological Reversal, the energetic chaos created by Neurological Disorganization also needs to be regulated before the energy system is open to influence. It is equivalent to lining up dominos in a knock-on-effect line. When the system is affected by confused signals, the dominos are scattered randomly in all directions. Consequently, you don't get very far!

Not all the causes for Neurological Disorganization are known, but stress, trauma and emotional overwhelm can all serve to upset the delicate polarity of the energy system. To correct this condition a technique called 'Collarbone Breathing', developed by Roger Callahan, may be used. It takes approximately two minutes to perform. The breathing exercise has a regulating quality that restores balance and organization to energy flow.

## COLLARBONE BREATHING

**1** Keeping both arms from touching the body. Place the index and middle fingers of your right hand on your right Collarbone point (*see* page 45). With the same two fingers of your left hand, tap the Gamut point of your right hand continuously as you:

- Breathe in half way and hold your breath for seven taps
- Breathe in fully and hold your breath for seven taps
- Breathe half way out and hold your breath for seven taps
- Breathe out fully and hold your breath for seven taps
- Breathe naturally for seven taps

**2** Now place the two fingers of your right hand on your left Collarbone point and repeat the breathing routine.

**3** Then bend the two fingers of your right hand double and place the knuckle joints on the right Collarbone Point and repeat the breathing routine.

**4** Repeat the same process with the right hand fingers for the left Collarbone point.

**5** The complete procedure is now repeated with the left hand.

This process should realign the imbalance caused by Neurological Disorganization, as well as promoting relaxation. Once the correction has been performed, reapply EFT for the issue that was formerly unresponsive.

## DEHYDRATION

Another condition that we have observed which affects success is dehydration. Water is a good conductor and cleanser of the system and is vital to all bodily functions. The positive effects of water are often over looked. Water is essential for every physical and chemical process that occurs within the body. Remarkably, nearly 80% of our body is made up of water. Every day we lose one and half litres of water through the skin. A lack of fluid in the system can produce a state of dryness on many levels. The telltale signs include dry skin, lack of perspiration, constipation, dry mouth and difficulty in expressing emotions, particularly crying. To ensure that your fluid intake is sufficient, make a practice of drinking at least eight glasses of water every day and a glass of water before each tapping session.

# HUMAN
## CONTACT

Difficult problems that are unresponsive can be resolved a lot easier when another person is present. The interaction of energy between two people can give extra potency to the treatment. If another person taps for you, they are essentially influencing your energy system with their own. As soon as they make contact, both your energy systems become intricately linked and connected. If Psychological Reversal is a problem, adding another person's healing energy to the equation can make all the difference.

If deep traumatic issues are involved, it is always better treated by a quali-fied practitioner. A practitioner is trained to detect emotionally charged statements, postures, facial signs and auditory clues that offer insight and guidance in the tapping routines. They will also be able to identify possible energy states that are preventing the process from working. Forming a trust-ing relationship can encourage the emotional safety required when facing extremely scary or painful issues. They will be able to take you through the experience quickly and with minimal distress, as well as giving you the support that is vital in these circumstances.

# PERSISTENCE

A little persistence goes a long way. You may find that you need to apply EFT to a problem for a prolonged period before the energy system is able to sustain the required changes. Most of us want quick fixes and instant cures to our problems and EFT is usually able to oblige. However, some difficulties need extra tapping sessions to remove the negative effects per-manently. Equally, physical or chronic conditions respond best to a daily schedule of tapping. You wouldn't expect EFT to resolve a chronic health complaint in one session any more than you would expect one painkiller to work indefinitely. Apply the technique persistently to whatever problem you are struggling with until you gain the relief you require.

## Chapter 16

# Working with a Therapist

Life's challenges can be overwhelming at times. One of the first things you realize as you begin using EFT is that you are taking back your own inherent power. However, there may be certain problems that you feel unable to work through on your own, such as when you are coming to terms with deeply emotive memories, and so you may wish to consult an EFT practitioner. We recommend that you seek professional guidance when addressing any trauma or intense emotion that is likely to be overwhelming.

## THE ROLE OF AN EFT PRACTITIONER

- A practitioner has a trained ear for picking up important beliefs and statements that you could otherwise miss. They are also qualified to detect visual and auditory signs of energetic disruption, so they are able to instruct you when to tap.
- Difficult problems can greatly benefit from someone else administering the treatment for you. This allows you to remain focused on the problem, while the practitioner concentrates on

balancing the energetic disturbances. This will also ensure that the process runs much more smoothly, as well as taking less time.

- Unlike other therapeutic approaches, an EFT practitioner interjects every time an emotion surfaces. They do not expect a client to stew in their emotions. You do not need to re-experience painful or traumatic emotions, just name them. An emotion is tapped away as soon as it's encountered. This ensures a minimal amount of distress during the treatment. Once all the emotional landmines have been cleared, you are free to discover what there was to learn, unhindered.
- If you keep going round in circles, sabotaging your own efforts to overcome a problem, a therapist can often help break the unhealthy pattern.
- As a non-judgemental observer, a therapist can help identify and offer insight into core issues.
- An EFT session can be content free – meaning you can keep your problems secret if you wish, even from the therapist. You do not need to disclose the circumstances or emotions you experience. As long as your thoughts are tuned into the memories you wish to clear, the emotions can be tapped away without encroaching on your privacy, while still receiving the vital support and reassurance of the practitioner.

emotional healing

- A therapist will also provide you with a safe and comfortable healing environment when working on very painful issues.
- Ultimately, an EFT therapist will facilitate your journey into self-awareness.

## QUESTIONS TO ASK

Before receiving help from a practitioner there will be a number of questions that you will want to ask. These may include:

- What experience do they have with cases such as yours?
- How long have they been practising?
- How many sessions may be required?
- How much do they charge?
- What qualifications do they have?
- Do you provide free preliminary consultations?
- Are telephone consultations available? (The answer to this is 'yes', it is possible to have sessions with a therapist over the phone.)

# VISITING
## A THERAPIST

We sometimes ask our clients to bring a shopping list of problems with them to the consultation. This is useful in a number of ways. It helps them to see what they want to address in the sessions and what is most important for them to clear. It is also a healing process to write feelings down before using EFT, as it helps to focus where you have come from and where you wish to go.

Once the cloudy emotions are out the way, you can gain in-depth clarity into your situation. By recording your feelings prior, during and after the session, you can benefit from a deeper understanding, enabling you to gain wisdom from your experience. It is also useful to see the contrast in perspective that occurs before and after tapping.

## What happens in an EFT session?

- We begin by taking a case history and informing the client that all sessions are confidential.
- We talk a little about how EFT works.
- We illustrate the location of the tapping points and ask permission to tap on the client.
- We explain that we may interrupt the client if they begin to get emotional while talking about their difficulty. We then tap all negative emotions away until they are completely calm and ready to continue.
- If the client feels nervous or apprehensive about the session, we begin by tapping away these feelings.

emotional healing

- The client is asked to tell us what they would like our help with.
- All statements that carry any negative emotions are written down by the therapist along with the SUD score (*see* page 64). After tapping, these statements and SUD scores are re-checked to see if any emotion remains, and tapped for as necessary.
- If the client wishes to tell their story once all negative emotions are tapped away, they are encouraged to do so. We follow the client's lead and respect their wishes.
- EFT sessions typically come to a natural close.
- The client is encouraged to tap at home and given handouts explaining the EFT procedure.

The next three cases are all taken from our own practice. They are more in-depth and complicated than the usual self-help issues. All of the clients mentioned experiencing extreme emotions, which would have been very difficult for them to resolve on their own. We have included them as examples of when to work with a therapist.

### beverley's story – overwhelming grief

Beverley came across EFT at an extremely vulnerable point in her life. She was in a state of turmoil, with a great number of emotional demands being placed upon her.

'I first met Val and Paul in September 1999. This was at the same time as my mother was diagnosed with lung cancer, which totally devastated me. I had reached an all-time low on the emotional front. I could not stop crying and was not coping with coming to terms with my mother's illness.

'Booking myself an appointment was the best decision I ever made. Once there, Val asked me to rate the scale of my emotional intensity out of ten. I can honestly say that nothing was below a ten. After the tapping was performed I felt so much better and was able to talk about my mother without constantly bursting into tears.

'I was so impressed that I decided to attend one of their self-help workshops so that when different emotions arose I could deal with them. When my sister came to visit she was astonished how relaxed I appeared. I had been using the technique before she arrived, so not only had I benefited but also I was able to be a great support to the rest of the family.

'Sadly, my mother died in the following January. On the day of her funeral, I wasn't coping at all and knew that as soon as the hearse arrived I was going to fall apart. I phoned Val and she immediately began to work with me over the phone. I was impressed how effective EFT really was. When the hearse finally arrived, I was able to go outside and look at the flowers surrounding my mother's coffin. There is no way I could have done this without EFT, it enabled me to cope and reduced my overwhelming feelings. My grief remained at a manageable level. For this I am extremely grateful.'

The next case was very lengthy. We needed to perform over 30 different tapping rounds to eradicate the feelings that had resulted from a traumatic incident in Irene's past. It would have been very difficult for her to approach this problem on her own and we would definitely not recommend treating this level of trauma without a qualified practitioner to help you. Here is Irene's story, in her own words.

### irene's story – the secret

'I was very frightened about how I would cope when my secret was unearthed. I had never mentioned this episode of my life to anyone before, as it was too frightening and shameful to relate.

'I began to re-run the chain of events that occurred on that summer's day, decades ago, to Val. I was a young girl ten years old, playing happily in the local field with my friend Dawn. We hadn't been there long when we felt someone behind us. As we spun round to see who had sneaked up on us, there stood a man we didn't know. He began talking to us. He pointed towards a tent in the distance and said that it belonged to him and invited us to come over and have a look. I wished he would leave us alone and I suddenly became very scared. He continued to talk, urging us towards the tent, it turned out that he was a solider on leave. We thought that if we walked along with him, once we got to the tent we could quickly run past and go straight back home.

'We were told to sit down. He became persistent with his pleading for us to come inside and see his knife and gun. It seemed as if we'd been there for ages and while he relayed his stories of war we didn't dare move or speak to each other. I remained glued to the ground, too frightened to get up and run away. I just smiled weakly, even as he started to molest me.

'He kept saying I should come into his tent because he had something he wanted to show me. He produced his knife and started telling more war stories. Any time now, I thought, he was going to use the knife on me. Suddenly, I saw Dawn's father running over towards us. He had seen what was going on and looked very concerned. The solider quickly put his knife away and went inside the tent to hide. By now, Dawn's father was screaming and shouting and running as fast as he could. Mistakenly, we thought he was cross with us and we became even more frightened.

'Once upon us, he threatened the soldier and told him he was going to get the police. I was petrified that the solider would bring out his gun, so I just sat perfectly still, shaken by the whole ordeal. The molester ran off, leaving everything behind.

'We did not speak the entire way home. Neither of us told her dad what had happened or how scared we had been. He didn't ask either – there was just this dreadful silence. When I got home, I was so confused. I knew I should tell my mum, but somehow I couldn't bring myself to. I felt ashamed and thought that I had done wrong. So I kept quiet. It was never mentioned, by me or anyone else, until now. I had kept it all a secret for nearly 40 years.

'The EFT session with Val was a mammoth one, lasting well over two hours. Every emotional memory was neutralized in turn. I cried tears of grief, shame, humiliation and anger throughout, but I was so glad to finally let it all go. At last, I'd been helped to release the torrid emotions that had been connected to that horrendous experience.

'Now, I can tell anyone about that time without any hang-ups. I can speak about it quite comfortably without an emotional reaction. Everything has been released and I feel totally different.

Thank goodness for EFT. I think it would have taken me much longer to unravel and come to terms with, if I had tried a different approach.'

As Irene relayed her story, Val deliberately stopped her at every significant point and neutralized the current emotion. This procedure ensures that the overall trauma is weakened at each step along the way. As this occurs, the link between certain scenes in her mind and the resulting emotional responses are broken. As the links diminish, the emotional energy is easy to clear away. Once completed, we double-check that she can recall the series of events without experiencing any distress.

We have illustrated this process in the last case. We have highlighted in italics each phrase which caused our next client, June, emotional distress and when treatment was applied. This approach helps to save any additional pain from being experienced. Every time a memory is recollected that evokes an emotional response, we immediately tapped to minimize the client's suffering.

### june's story – miscarriage

June wrote us an account of her rather intense EFT session. She was a 45-year-old single mum, with a son aged 11. She was still having difficulty coming to terms with the loss of her baby many years before. Over the hour, she recalled the whole experience.

'Until finding EFT, I had been carrying a lot of guilt inside for 20 years. Once I arrived, I explained that when I was 24 I had become pregnant. Although I continually experienced problems with the pregnancy, I was repeatedly told everything was OK. After six months, I needed to see the doctor again because I was in a lot of pain and had been bleeding. My doctor was away, so I saw a locum instead. After discovering that I had been bleeding through the entire pregnancy, he decided that I should go into to hospital for a scan. I was admitted the same day.

'While having the scan, the nurse *continually turned her back to me* in order to talk to her colleague about their working hours when she was supposedly watching the monitor screen. I thought, because she was talking, it indicated how easy it was to take a scan and that if there were any problems they would be obvious. The scan results came back normal and I was duly discharged after three days.

'A week later, I woke up in the middle of the night and *thought I had wet myself*. However, when I went to the toilet I noticed a green discharge. I called the doctor and he immediately sent me back to hospital. At the hospital, *I was informed that I had gone into labour.* They explained that my waters had broken and that the green discharge was a sign that *my baby was in distress.* The doctors decided to give me a drug that would stop the labour.

'The next morning I was still in labour. As I was only 26 weeks pregnant, it was explained to me that *the chances of survival for the baby were very slim* and even if they could save the baby, the *likelihood of brain damage was high*. The labour continued until lunchtime, when my baby was born.

'*The baby was immediately rushed away* before I had even chance to see it. *I didn't even know whether I had given birth to a boy or girl*. After a phone call, I was informed that it was a girl. There was another woman giving birth in the next room, but her baby cried as it was born. *All I can remember was the utter silence of mine.*

'After about ten minutes, *I was told that my baby girl had died*. I was put in a side room, away from all the other mothers and *left alone with my husband*. He finally went home, as *he didn't know what to do or say to me*. In all my confusion and despair *I never thought to ask where my baby was or what they had done with her*. No-one offered to tell me either. *I could not have a birth certificate*, because it was classed as a miscarriage, even though she was alive at birth. I was not given any counselling and *was sent home the same day "to get on with my life"*.

'The midwife, who called a few days later, told me that *"I should think myself lucky, as I could always have other children, unlike some women"*. *I felt really low* and put on a great deal of weight over the next six weeks. When I went to the doctor for my check up, he grabbed my stomach and pulled up the flab saying, that *it was about time I lost all this fat!*

'I had kept all the feelings of *hurt, guilt, pain, humiliation, total despair and loss* bottled up inside for the last 20 years, as *no-one had wanted to help me*. I eventually divorced my husband three years later, as he would not help me and inevitably the marriage was doomed. *I always felt guilty,* often thinking I could of done more to save my daughter and that *maybe she would have survived if only I had tried harder.*

'I worked through the emotions surrounding my daughter's death throughout the session, clearing the traumatic memories and distressing emotions, one after another. We covered many aspects that arose from the situation, from *the doctor's attitude*, to my *guilt feelings*, the *grief* and even *my husband's lack of support*. Finally, I was able to let go and forgive myself. I will never forget that awful experience but it doesn't plague me anymore. I can now look forward, rather than back.'

Working with a therapist can produce profound changes and insights which might take longer to achieve on your own. If you are apprehensive about working on your issue without support, or just prefer to work with a therapist, a list of contact numbers can be found at the back of this book.

# Afterword

The presence of a doctor, listening and giving advice in a caring way, can be very therapeutic when one is in an afflicted or weakened state. They provide a welcome tonic, to uplift us, in our hour of need. But, due to growing demand from an ever-increasing population and an alarming lack of resources, it is no longer possible for a doctor to give this kind of caring attention to everyone. Often ten minutes is the extent of the time that they can practically offer.

It is apparent that we must do everything within our power to provide a healing environment for ourselves and our loved ones. We must endeavour to care for our body and mind as never before in order to maintain optimum health. We are being handed back some of the responsibility for caring for ourselves.

We believe that The Emotional Freedom Technique is a divine gift, offered unselfishly through the healing hands of Gary Craig and Roger Callahan. With a gift this good, we are convinced that we have a real opportunity to heal ourselves, as well as others.

For the first time in decades, a technique has been discovered that can be applied universally to all emotional problems. It is a therapy that focuses on the area where thoughts, energy and emotion overlap and it offers a new way to achieve emotional fulfilment. This form of Energy Psychology could revolutionize current practice. EFT is a valuable addition to any therapist's healing tools and we predict that in the future this technique, and others like it, will be taken up by many health professionals – alternative and ortho-dox alike.

In our quest to help others, we have explored and become proficient in many disciplines over the years. EFT is the answer we were searching for – a quick, gentle, yet effective method that can offer rapid relief from emo-tional distress. An holistic approach with no harmful side-effects that is easy to learn and that everybody can benefit from; a technique which can release the pain from our past, remove life-restricting limitations and phobias, improve our relationships, relieve aches and pains, diffuse volatile emotions and help us to move confidently towards the future.

Throughout this book we have made some extraordinary claims. Yet, time and again we have witnessed amazing results. Now we have learnt to trust in EFT and have come to expect the high success rate that we now currently experience.

We are still only scratching the surface of future possibilities and the full impact of this discovery is yet to come. Research and clinical trials are cur-rently taking place all around the world to improve understanding of the meridian system and illustrate the effectiveness of EFT. However, you should now know everything you need to produce the same results as the ones we have described in this book. We hope that you will benefit, as we have, from the emotional freedom that EFT offers.

# Glossary

**Acupressure or Acupuncture Point** – A term used within Chinese Medicine to refer to the points on the body located along the meridians that act as gateways or amplifiers to the energy system.

**Apex Effect** – A common response to treatment in which improvement is not acknowledged or where another unrelated factor is seen as responsible for the beneficial changes.

**Aspects** – The different elements to any given problem – physical or emotional.

**EFT** – Emotional Freedom Technique. Gary Craig's simplified tapping technique derived from Dr Roger Callahan's 'Thought Field Therapy'.

**Energy Toxins** – A form of energy pollution that can block the successful outcome of EFT or any other treatment. Energy toxins can include any substance that is ingested, absorbed or present within the environment.

**Gamut Point** – An acupressure point on the back of the hand, which is tapped while performing eye movements that balance the left and right side of the brain.

**Generalization Effect** – Several issues can often be addressed through neutralizing one key problem or root core issue.

**Kinesiology** – A diagnostic treatment using muscle testing to attain information from the unconscious mind and the body's innate intelligence.

**Neurological Disorganization** – A term derived from Kinesiology referring to a confused energy state which can reduce the effectiveness of tapping procedures.

**Psychological Reversal** – A form of polarity reversal within the energy system that is seen as the cause of all Self-Sabotage. Psychological Reversal can prevent conventional and holistic treatments from working.

**SUDS Level** (Subjective Units of Disturbance or Discomfort Scale) – A measurement of emotional or physical discomfort scored on a scale of one to ten. It is used to monitor progress and help in combating the Apex Effect.

**TFT** (Thought Field Therapy) – The original discovery of Roger Callahan in which combinations and specific sequences of tapping points are used. EFT is a simplified modification of Thought Field Therapy.

**VOC Scale** (Validity of Cognition Scale) – A score given out of ten pertaining to the level of belief or truth in a statement.

# Resources

**The Heart Centre**
Val and Paul Lynch
75 Anderida Road
Lower Willingdon
Eastbourne
East Sussex BN22 OQB

Tel: 01323 505263 (office hours)
E-mail: **heartcentre@tesco.net** (for training enquiries, bookings, individual
and telephone consultations)
Web site: **www.the-heart-centre.com** (contains articles, information, case
histories, and details of training and workshops)

**Emotional Freedom Techniques™**
Gary H. Craig
P.O. Box 398
The Sea Ranch, CA 95497

Tel: (707) 785 2848
Web site: **www.emofree.com** (contains articles, information, resources,
case histories, links, e-mail forum)

**Callahan Techniques Ltd.**
Dr. Roger Callahan
78-816 Via Carmel
La Quinta, CA 92253

Tel: 760 564 1008
Web site: **www.tftx.com** (contains articles, books, research, products.)

**Energy Diagnostic & Treatment Methods (EdxTM)**
Fred P. Gallo, Ph.D.
40 Snyder Road
Hermitage, PA 16148

Web Site: **www.energypsych.com**

# About the Authors

**Val Lynch** runs The Heart Centre in Eastbourne, where she offers spiritual and personal discovery groups and holds regular workshops and courses on a wide variety of subjects. She is a qualified Holistic Counsellor, Professional Healer and Reiki Master. As an EFT practitioner, she sees clients on a one-to-one basis as well as facilitating training for therapists. Val has found EFT extremely beneficial within her group work and personal life. Through the application of EFT she has been able to attain emotional freedom as well as fulfil many of her own dreams.

**Paul Lynch** has been involved in self-development for many years, initially to overcome his own intense shyness. Not content with the laborious methods available, he sought a faster and more effective solution. As a result, Paul trained in NLP with founder, Richard Bandler, soon after he was introduced to EFT. He was so impressed with the ease and effectiveness of this technique that he became a practitioner. He has now made it his personal quest to bring this approach to others. Paul trains therapists in the use of EFT and presents self-help workshops with his wife Val.

# Index

emotional healing

emotional healing